Pasta and Pizza

Pasta and Pizza

Franco La Cecla

Translated by Lydia G. Cochrane

PRICKLY PARADIGM PRESS
CHICAGO

© 2007 Franco LaCecla
All rights reserved.

Prickly Paradigm Press, LLC
5629 South University Avenue
Chicago, Il 60637

www.prickly-paradigm.com

ISBN: 0-9794057-1-8
ISBN-13: 978-0-9794057-1-6
LCCN: 2007934316

Printed in the United States of America on acid-free paper.

Contents

Introduction: Our History *al dente*   i

I. The Invention of a Foodstuff Common to All Italians   1

II. Pasta and Pizza in the World: The Great Emigration   47

III. Childhood: A Digression   85

IV. Eating and Thinking Like an Italian   91

Selected Bibliography   117

Additional Bibliography   121

Guaje e mmaccarune
Se magnano caude.
(Misfortunes and macaroni should be eaten hot.)
—Giambattista Basile
Lo cunto de' li cunti, 1636, IV.3

Introduction
Our History *al dente*

I have become accustomed to eating pasta at least five times a week, and since I travel between Germany and Mexico, this can create problems. So I have researched how to translate *al dente* in other languages, and I have discovered that in no language but Italian is there an expression that fits this concept.

> —Ivan Illich, *contribution to an open seminar, Oratorio Domenicano, Pistoia, 25 May 1997*

How does it happen that Italians eat pasta and pizza? Or, rather, How did pasta and pizza become the typical Italian dishes, to the point of merging with the Italian character, not only internally, as Italians view one another, but also—and especially—from abroad, as the foreigner sees Italians as a human group clearly distinct from other groups?

It may seem that simply asking these questions pushes the Italian identity to the limits of banality, to a reductive and prosaic stereotype, but it would be just as dangerous to forget about identity—that strange face with humble but pervasive features that a culture creates for itself or accepts from the outside.

Anthropology has taught us to take seriously the banal events of everyday life—from people's dress to their gestures, from the ways they look right or left to whether they eat noisily or silently—and it has helped us to discover that these things, along with language, are what makes up the culture of a specific human group.

The Italy made up of saints, navigators, and poets and the Italy of the Renaissance, great paintings, and other works of art, is undeniably a complex recognizable for its humanistic patrimony. But we need to remember that such an image, although an enormously successful reconstruction of the Italian past, is a high-culture facade that may crumble the minute it fails to include the common man's capacity for inventing a more domestic, "down to earth" image of Italians and Italianness.

This slim volume is an attempt to pay homage to the extraordinary talent for invention that has contributed, as we shall see, to the recent discovery of the nature of Italians. In this operation food—what Italians eat in order to *feel themselves Italian*—has been as important as, if not more than, the Renaissance, Michelangelo, Donatello, Leopardi, and Manzoni. It pains me to say so, but behind the apparent triviality of the culture of foodstuffs there lurks one of the most successful propaganda operations carried on by a people in recent world history.

That operation has characteristics so original that they often escape analysis. Above all, we contemporary Italians are unable to look at ourselves and question what we believe to be our normal manner of being, which we assume to have existed for ever. Today's Italians have completed the job of wiping out the incredible efforts to create "Italianness" of the generations before them. It was an operation carried out by the lowly artisans of daily life: not by the artists, writers, and politicians, but by shopkeepers and workers, fathers and housewives, and, above all, by the twenty-seven million Italians who left Italy during the last century to live in a far-off land.

Italianness is also (and to a great extent) the face that Italians established for themselves elsewhere. The history of the creation of that image is still to be written, but the present text hopes to make a contribution in that direction. It should be understood that to speak of an "invention of Italianness" in no way implies that Italy does not exist nor that Italianness is a mystification at the expense of local or regional interests. To the contrary, all cultural identities (localism included) are an invention, the reinterpretation of scattered evidence from the past and the present organized as a tradition.

Cultural, ethnic, or national identity is an interesting and potentially perilous game that human groups launch to draw the group together, forge ahead, and become recognizable, both to themselves and to others. It is a formidable and at times an essential instrument, but it has no intrinsic value as an instrument: it remains a process in fieri and is of service as long as it is useful. It would be a mistake to think it a value immune to the capacity of persons and human groups to adapt, transform themselves, mix, or "creolize." But it would be equally mistaken to think that it should not be taken seriously.

Italianness, as a construction of the collective imaginary, is a total social fact (*à la* Durkheim), as are the language that we speak, our hand gestures, and the way we move our haunches when we walk. It has no "author" except the multitude because it is created between the kitchen and the chair placed outside the front door to watch the passers-by; between the town square, the post office, and the railroad station; in the holds of the ships bound for America; and a part of the Sunday stroll along the village street. A culture, viewed as a datum related to people, is a complex system of recall and variation; an elaboration that requires the habitual and unconscious practice of no longer wondering why.

The present work, on the other hand, is an unnatural attempt to ask why. Why *do we eat the way we do*? But also Why *do we talk as we eat*, to the point of telling our children to do just that? *We are what we eat* and *we eat what we are*.

The text that follows arises from a desire to do justice to the anonymous Italianness of the Italians, a quality so different from all other anonymous identities that it is recognizable wherever it exists.

Pasta and pizza are a pretext for talking about a history that is both circumstantial and intelligible and for considering the unique and collective capacity of Italians—peninsular and insular—to invent themselves and present themselves by means of odd-shaped edible objects that may be long, short, round, solid, tubular, and even flat. Here is where, more than anywhere else, Italians have found the theater for their recent history.

Instructions for Use: This is Not a Cookbook

But then what is it? It is an attempt to reason before a mirror and set a distance between the self and the mirror image. The reader should not expect recipes or cooking times, which is a shame, because there is no cuisine without them. If we look in a bookstore for a book about pasta or pizza, we find hundreds of them, all with lovely illustrations, but few of them attempt to explain that before pasta and pizza are a recipe, they are a mentality, a specific way of conceiving of taste and savor. Cookbooks all lie to some extent, because they seek to systematize a highly fluid matter better suited to being spoken about, one person to another, in front of a stove: the moment that matter is written down it is reduced to a still-life. Perhaps some day someone will write about the close similarity between the still-life as a genre and cookbook illustrations. Not by chance, the succulent plates prepared for such illustrations are tossed out after being photographed because the food is lacquered, greased, and sprinkled with strange liquids to bring out highlights and colors, hence it is inedible. There are cooks who cook only for food photographers and photographers who specialize in foodstuffs.[1] The difference between a culture of foodstuffs and a book of recipes is similar to the difference between a living language and a somewhat boring grammar book.

---

[1] I can think of only one exception to this rule: Franco Zecchin's photographs for Anna Tasca Lanza's *The Heart of Sicily: Recipes and Reminiscences of Regaleali, a Country Estate*, which show plates of food as a contextual and living part of the landscape, on a par with farmyards, fields, and peasants.

Cookbooks are part of a process that tends to freeze foodstuffs within a given moment of their cultural history (which makes them excellent historical documents). This "Bird's Eye" operation hinders the transmission of the gastronomic knowledge that every culture possesses.

There are secrets, gestures, obsessions, and atmospheres that can only be learned from peeling potatoes, shelling beans, salting eggplant slices, canning a sauce, lopping off the ends of a cucumber and rubbing the top over the rest of the cucumber to take away the bitter taste, putting food in the pot to boil "without looking at it"—all operations that require a good dose of domestic superstition to be carried out properly. It may be unnecessary to mention it, but cooking is a direct descendant of magic and alchemy, and the plumes of steam, the flames, and the clouds of smoke that gather in the hood over the stove are signs of our ties with alcoves where earthy materials boil, coagulate, and break free, metamorphosing and transforming the world.

The text that follows is divided into three parts, as I have chosen to talk about pasta and pizza against three backgrounds: Italy in formation, Italy in the world, and Italian cooking compared with other cuisines, cultures, and tastes. I have consulted a variety of sources and works, and I will let them speak for themselves in the text. Some topics are poorly documented: for example, nearly all recent books about pasta refer to Emilio Sereni's essay, "Ii napoletani da 'mangiafolglia' a 'mangiamaccheroni,'" a work written in the 1970s, but that offers insights that remain unequaled. The present work follows Sereni's notion that major changes in the alimentation of a people correspond to broader changes and cataclysms. As Sereni wrote in "Note di storia dell'alimentatazione nel Mezzogiorno":

> Reasons of space prevent us from taking up in this note the broader theme of the origins and the history of pasta products in Italy, a topic that as of now lacks an overall treatment. We will limit our remarks here to presenting materials for a history of the true and proper revolution in the alimentation of the southern populations, which made Naples the capital of macaroni and which presents, it seems to us—when we consider that gastronomic revolution in relation to the entire evolution of agriculture, urbanism, and society in the Mezzogiorno—an inherent interest not only for folkloristic curiosity, but also for historiographical studies.

A culture's vitality is expressed by its ability to invent a cuisine that responds to changing ecological and economic situations, but that vitality is sustained by symbolic and gastronomic motivations that tend to run counter to the simple, mechanical functionality of change. As social history has taught us in recent years, it is the redefinition of the structures of everyday life that provides a creative interpretation of the conditions and constrictions of history. A genuine history and an anthropology of Italian cooking remains unwritten, however. One of the reasons for this is that the culture of alimentation is still so alive among Italians that it seems useless to write its history. We stand between a love for a patrimony that we feel is slipping from our grasp and a respect for structures of daily life in continual renewal.

It is certain that something is disappearing. The great African writer Amadou Hampaté Bâ said about oral culture in a speech before a UNESCO meeting in 1960: "In Africa, every time an old man dies a library burns down." Similarly, when an Italian grandmother dies, we realize that with her we have lost a wealth of stories (not recipes, but narrations about how things are done), an orality of gestures, and a pragmatics of explanations that no transcription and no book is capable of capturing.

This book exists thanks to the insistence of Lucetta Scaraffia and Ernesto Galli della Loggia, to whom I owe the pleasure of discovering the seriousness of this topic. To Piero Zanini, his tireless genius for rummaging, and his skill as an investigator I owe many of the details related here. I also owe a debt to Giannino Malossi for our highly enjoyable discussions of the connection between pop culture and fashion, America and Italy, and the conviction that the two lands are a strange reflection of one another. Loretta D'Orsogna has provided me with a plunge into her roots in America and Abruzzo and the evidence that Italy is a country that exists to a great extent abroad. Leonardo Soresi has given me inside information about pasta-making that could come only from a son of the art. Gian-Paolo Biasin has offered me reassurances and helpful information on California based on his teaching of Italianness there. He also introduced me to Alan Dundees, whose talent bridges the gap between humor and the appetite, in Italy and abroad. Gigi in the

Libreria Patagonia in Venice provided an early spur to write this book and provided me with precious details on the Sicilian origin of many things. I hope he likes the book. Finally, I owe much to all those with whom, some years ago, I organized a conference with the title of "Cavoli a merenda" (Cabbage for a Snack), focused on encounters and clashes between cultures through foods: Jack Goody, Igor De Garines, John Simmoons, Claude Fishler, Lucetta Scaraffia, Francesca Isidori, Giulia Sissa, Anna Foa, Altan Gokalp, David Kubiak, and Luigi Veronelli.

I
The Invention of a Foodstuff Common to All Italians

Italian Unity, dreamed of by the fathers of the Risorgimento, is today called *pastasciutta*; this is why not much blood has been shed, but lots of *pummarola* sauce.
>   —Cesare Marchi, *Quando siamo a tavola*

It's not a matter of dividing Italy geographically. Rather, it is a question of returning to the values that can unite it. And these are two: religion and *pastasciutta*.

>   —Giacomo Cardinal Biffi,
>   *to Johns Hopkins University students,*
>   *Bologna (paraphrased)*

On July 26, 1860, Camillo Benso, Count Cavour, sent a letter in which he used code and ironic humor to send a message. He states: "We second [your suggestion] regarding the Continent, given that the macaroni are not yet cooked, but as for the oranges, which are already on our table, we have every intention of eating them." The count, who was seeking to advance Italian unity, was communicating (in French) that the moment had not yet come for an attempted annexation of Naples (*les macaroni*), the capital of the Kingdom of the Two Sicilies, but that the time was ripe for Garibaldi's operation in Sicily (*les oranges*).

This means that one of the leading proponents of the political unity of the Italian Peninsula was arguing in highly picturesque alimentary terms. On closer analysis, Cavour's reasoning reveals a specific view of the Bel Paese of his day: Italy was a patchwork, even from the alimentary point of view. The quotation is cited by Alfredo Panzini, whose *Dizionario moderno delle parole che non si trovano nei dizionari comuni* was published in 1905, some forty-five years later. The entry "Maccheroni" also states: "Macaroni are very common in Naples, and, with green vegetables, they constitute the preferred food of the people, to the point that often the term is taken as equivalent to 'Neapolitan.'"

A hundred years after Cavour, the term *maccheroni* still seems to have been more local than Italian, but it was a sign of "modernity" to give it official status within the Italian language. After Cavour's letter, the Peninsula underwent a modernization that, from the political viewpoint, saw the emergence of the unified state and, from the cultural viewpoint, witnessed the slow construction of common reference points within the fragmented mosaic that Italy had been. Italy was a jigsaw puzzle to be reconstructed—or perhaps invented—on a new and unified base.

Part of that effort to recompose and invent Italy and Italianness was directed to the invention of foods common to all Italians. In fact—as Cavour was well aware —pasta was not consumed throughout Italy in 1860, and only some decades later did it (together with pizza, although with different symbolic components) become the logo, the coordinated image, the banner of Italy and the basic stereotype for recognizing Italians.

Pasta Before There Were Italians

But before pasta became Italians' most recognizable feature, diversity reigned. What was the alimentary situation in Italy in the latter half of the 1800s?

Thirty years after Cavour's letter, an Agrarian Inquiry reporting to the members of the new national Parliament on conditions in several largely rural provinces noted that pasta was not yet among the commonest types of food. In the administrative district of Gaeta—not a particularly depressed area in those same years—the Inquiry tells us that "pasta is rarely used, and meat much more rarely." According to Maurizio Sentieri, in the province of Trapani pasta and meat were consumed only on festive occasions.

What did Italians eat in those days—and we should remember that for the most part the population was rural? The answer is, very different things from one zone to another, and, even in the South, other things besides pasta. In *La terra e la luna* (1989), Paolo Camporesi states:

> Porridge, *pappa* (purée), soups, minestre boiled long and slowly over the fire have always made up the peasants' diet—the eternal whitish or greyish porridge made of inferior cereals (like the "beige" porridge of buckwheat). Only in the eighteenth century were these very gradually supplanted by the yellow polenta of maize.

All of these dishes were accompanied by bread, the *primary, essential, and fundamental element*, which was made from all available flours and, in hard times or periods of shortage, made with substitutes that could even be grasses, roots, and leaves. Only in the South, and not everywhere there, was wheat flour to be found. In 1877, Camporesi tells us, Sidney Sonnino, sent to the South to write up an agrarian investigation on the conditions of the peasants, declared:

> The peasant in Sicily eats bread made of wheat flour, and except for cases of extreme poverty they have enough nourishment, while the Lombard peasant eats almost exclusively maize, and suffers from physiological hunger even when his belly is full.

Emilio Sereni recalls, echoed by Camporesi, that this fragmentation was fairly long-established, given that Gabriele Fasano, in his *Tasso napoletano* of the late 1600s, lists epithets for the various peoples of Italy according to their customary foods: Lombards were *mangiarapi* (turnip-eaters); the peoples of the Tuscan-Emilian Appenines were *mazzamarroni* (chestnut-bashers); Cremonesi were *mangiafagioli* (bean-eaters); Abruzzesi, *pane unto* (oiled bread); Florentines *cacafagioli* (literally, beans shitters); and Neapolitans *cacafoglie* (leaf shitters) or *mangiafoglie* (leaf-eaters).

In *The Culture of Food*, a history of alimentation in Europe, Massimo Montanari states that until 1600 meat and greens were the principal foodstuffs, although present in different quantities and qualities on the tables of the rich and the poor. A significant change took place during the seventeenth century, when meat became scarce throughout Europe, thanks to the destruction of forests and an increase in population. At that point cereals substituted for meats, even in Naples.

In the sixteenth century, only the Sicilians deserved the epithet of *mangiamaccheroni*, a nickname that points to an unusual situation and variation from the norm. Montanari informs us that in Naples (where importations of pasta from Sicily seems to have begun only in the late 1400s), a 1509 law prohibited the production of "taralli, susamelli, ceppule, maccarune, trii vermicelli," or any other sort of pasta (except in case of need for the sick) at times when the price of wheat "rises as a result of war, famine, or inclement weather."

In Eclogue IV of his *Lo cunto de' li cunti*, a work published posthumously in 1636, Giambattista Basile states:

> tre so le cose che la casa strudeno,
> zeppole, pane caudo e maccarune.
> (Three things destroy a household: deep-fried dough balls, hot bread, and macaroni)

Thus those three foods that might bring ruin to a family were counted as luxuries.

Neapolitans ate a good deal of meat, garden vegetables, and cabbage. They were called "leaf-eaters," despite Cavour's disapproval but to Benedetto Croce's amusement. As Emilio Sereni reports in his "Note," Croce mentions a comedy written in 1569 that presents a succulent altercation between a Sicilian soldier, Fiacavento, and a Neapolitan gentleman, Cola Francisco, who trade insults, the Neapolitan calling the soldier a *mangiamaccheroni* and the Sicilian responding with *mangiafoglie.*

In short, pasta existed in Italy, but it was not widely consumed or low-priced. It was considered an exotic dish and a luxury. Massimo Montanari mentions the distinction, which remained essential, between fresh pasta and dried pasta. The first, a simple dough of flour, water, and egg, was made for domestic use and immediate consumption; the second was dried immediately after it was made, which means that it would keep for some time. Montanari states:

> The first of these [fresh pasta] is a food of ancient date, widespread among Mediterranean populations and also in other parts of the world, for instance China. Dry pasta is a more recent invention and has been attributed to Arab origin, the technique for drying being developed in order to supply provisions suitable for desert travel.

It has been remarked that the Arab world lacks the notion of pasta and even a term for it, calling pasta *makkaroni.* It is probable, however, that it was the Arabs in Sicily who invented it, given that the geographer Idrisi speaks of it in the twelfth century, mentioning the production of a small form of dried pasta called *itrija* in Trabia, a locality not far from Palermo. According to Montanari, Idrisi reports: "A great quantity of pasta is made and exported all over, to Calabria and to other Muslim and Christian lands; and many shiploads are sent."

Sereni tells us that a Syriac lexicographer, Bar Alì, uses the term *itriya* two centuries earlier, however:

"Itriya is a product made from bran, which is prepared like the weavings of the makers of reed mats, and which is then dried and cooked."[2]

Dried Pasta and its Advantages: Classical Roots and Arabo-Siculan Uses

Dried pasta was more widely used by those who traveled by sea or by people who needed to store foodstuffs in difficult times. Fresh pasta was a treat: the macaroni and gnocchi that roll down from mountains of cheese in the Italian Land of Plenty—the Paese di Bengodi—seem to be of this sort, as are the various types of filled and stuffed pasta, fried or boiled, or the sweets that fill the treatises on court cuisine. Fresh pasta is extremely ancient: we know that the Greeks and Romans kneaded flour and water and boiled up *lagane*, strips of fresh pasta very like our modern lasagne. Baked lasagna—*patina apiciana*—is attested in the most famous text on Roman gastronomy, that of Apicius (IV 2). Horace

---

[2] It seems that the etymology of *Itriya*, from *tria* or from *Ittrija*, derives either from the Arabic root *tari* (humid, fresh) or from the Syriac and Aramaic root *natar* (to conserve). The word *tria* was still in use until recently in some Sicilian localities, according to the *Vocabolario siciliano-italiano, attenente a... parecchie arti e ad alcuni mestieiri* of Giuseppe Perez: "*Tria bastarda*: a long, round [type of] pasta somewhat bigger than *sopracapellini*." Joan Corominas's *Diccionario etimológico* states that vermicelli are called *fidelli* in Genoa, *fedelini* elsewhere, *findeos* in Sardinian, *fideus* in Catalan, *fideos* in Castillian, and *fides* in Greek, all terms from the Arabic world. The word *maccheroni* derives instead from the Latin *maccare* (to crush, batter, or bruise), a reference to working the dough. In Sicily today pureed fava beans are still called a *macco*.

speaks of the dish, as do treatises from the colonies of Magna Grecia and Sicily. The treatise on gastronomy of Archestratus of Gela (fifth century BCE) repeatedly uses the expression *elkuein laganon* (roll out the dough).

Camporesi tells us that in the nineteenth century fresh pasta was served in Emilia and Lombardy on certain holidays and special occasions. *Pasta fresca* often helped to celebrate a birth or console the bereaved after a death. It has much less to do with Italian Unity or the invention of Italianness, however: the pasta that interests us in that context is the dry variety, by its nature much less elite. Until the late seventeenth century in Naples and until the late nineteenth century in the Peninsula as a whole, even the dried variety was considered a luxury and a treat, as we have seen.[3]

Dried pasta first came from Sicily under Arab domination. At the time Sicily was a land in which durum wheat (*grano duro*) was cultivated "for ideological reasons," in the sense that it was grown with no thought of commercial ends but only for personal use and for connections with Arabic medicine of the ninth century, which focused on opposing Arabic knowledge and that of the Greek Hippocratic tradition. The Arabs admiringly adopted the alimentary schemes of Hippocrates, including wheat bread. For the Arabs of Sicily, alimentation was closely connected to medicine

---

[3]There is disagreement regarding the question, however. Sereni rightly observes that we should not believe that names like *mangiafolia* and *mangiamaccheroni* conceal a granitic truth. These were cultural stereotypes that concealed differences that were never quite so neat. Thus the expression, "like cheese on macaroni" (*come il cacio sui maccheroni*) was so common in Naples in the mid-1500s that Giordano Bruno says in his *Spaccio*, "the macaroni fell, as the proverb goes in Naples, into the cheese."

and agriculture, as attested in the *Book of Agriculture* of Ibn Al Aww m (ninth century). In the same century, Paolo Scarpi tells us, the "Mediterranean diet" came into being and spread throughout the Mediterranean Basin, returning to an idea of a civilization derived from the cereal and wine revolution.

A like pairing of Dionysos and Demeter is praised in Plato's *Republic*, where the ideal life is led by those who consume vegetable products and cheeses and drink wine in moderation, thus going through life in peace and good health to a ripe old age. That life stood opposed to the ways of the Barbarians, who lacked civilization and did not possess Dionysos and Demeter, wine or cereals.

The Mediterranean diet is founded on this ideal. As is usually the case, it is not simply an alimentary regime, but also a norm, a discourse directed at the living regarding what is just, good, and fine. It would be a serious mistake to forget that pasta derives from that concept of a Mediterranean identity. The success of pasta in the second half of the nineteenth century and its "ideological" establishment—at first timidly, then increasingly—as the ideal food of Italians was the way Northern Italy (not the Arabs, this time) interpreted the Mediterranean character.

Cavour's metaphor of macaroni and oranges was not a chance phrase. It echoed a discourse about Italianness as Mediterraneanness. Moreover, the Mille —Garibaldi's thousand or so red-shirted volunteers— did much to further that operation, even in the alimentary area. But I am getting ahead of myself, and of Sicily and its pasta in the thirteenth century.

In the sixteenth century Sicily was still a place where macaroni was consumed, though to what extent is unclear. Both Sereni and Massimo Alberini tell us of a Sicilian holy man, Guglielmo Cuffitella of Scicli, who died in 1377 and whose beatifications proceedings (held in Palermo in 1537-38) mention miracles involving macaroni, although we cannot tell for sure whether the term refers to fresh or dried pasta.

In one miracle, "invitaverat Guillelmum aliquando compater suus Guiccioniius ad prandium, eique apposuerat maccarones seu lagana." Guiccione, a friend of Guglielmo's, invites the latter to dinner. Guiccione's wife, who detests the holy man, prepares *maccarones seu lagana*—macaroni or lasagna.

The pasta served to the hermit is full of husks and inedible bits. Guglielmo says nothing, and blesses the food. When he urges the spiteful wife and her husband to taste the dish, the *lagana* are filled with delectable ricotta cheese. On another occasion, Guglielmo is invited to join Guiccione and his wife but remains at home, so Guiccione sends a boy to the holy man's house—it is Ash Wednesday—with a bowl of hot lasagna. Guiccione's wife has instructed the boy to hide the bowl in the cupboard. Lent goes by, and Guiccione wonders why his bowl has not been returned. When the boy arrives at his door to ask for it, Guglielmo pretends to be astonished, opens the closet, and there is the lasagna, bubbling hot as if just taken out of the oven.

Sicilian dried pasta spread elsewhere. Genoese merchants became the main link for its diffusion in Northern Italy, and in the twelfth century Liguria and northern Tuscany become production zones for vermicelli and other types of pasta. Recipes for *tria* in four-teenth-century cookbooks call it a Genoese dish. In the fifteenth century pasta appears in Puglia, Provence, and England. In places where dried pasta was produced it may have been a humble foodstuff for the common people, but only up to a certain point, given that the earliest known document in Italian that mentions pasta is an act drawn up by a notary, Ugolino Scarpa, dated 2 February 1279, listing a box of macaroni among the goods that a soldier named Ponzio Bastone left to his heirs.

Alberini and Sereni both report that dried pasta became ordinary fare (rather than an occasional extravagance) only around 1630. By then meat consumption had diminished, with cereals taking its place. Above all, wider use of kneading machines and the invention of a mechanical press brought on a minor technological revolution that reduced the production cost of macaroni and other types of pasta.

The Neapolitan Revolution

In his essay on the history of alimentation in Naples Emilio Sereni describes the incredible revolution brought on by the adoption of macaroni. In the mid-1600s Naples was a very big city (population ca. 300,000), and the typical Neapolitan diet was meat and *foglia*—cabbage, salads, and greens. This diet was about to change drastically.

This was the Naples of Masaniello and his people's insurrection of 1647; a city heavily taxed by its

Aragonese rulers, where only a century earlier (when the population was around 220,000) the city butchered 20,000 cows, 10,000 calves, and 12,000 young steers per year—that is, one cow for every eleven Neapolitans, one calf for every twenty-two, and one young steer for every eighteen—an extraordinary figure by our modern criteria, if we consider that in 1934 the figure was one cow per ninety-seven inhabitants. The Neapolitans' former meat-and-greens diet provided nourishment, protein, and fiber; moreover, it produced a feeling of fullness, thanks to the water contained in the *foglie*. When Naples could no longer maintain this diet, it carried out an extraordinary revolution. Emilio Sereni tells us:

> This manifestation of the genius of the Neapolitans, in the solution of a complex problem of logistics, economics, and the supervision of food distribution, was by no means spontaneous, but rather emerged gradually, under pressure from worsening poverty.

The solution to finding a balanced diet was to top macaroni with cheese. Sereni continues:

> Apart from the energy-giving hydrocarbons that they contained, macaroni provided (at a level noticeably higher than bread) fiber in the form of vegetable protein, which cannot totally replace meat protein. Sprinkling pasta with cheese—which became the rule in the latter half of the 1600s—gave a supplement of animal protein and fats that came close to making a plate of macaroni a complete meal capable of providing (although at a much lower level than a meat diet) the alimentary mass and the

energy-giving materials and fiber necessary to maintain even a famished populace above the level of physiological starvation.

This is how Naples brought its masses into the modern age. The city's population remained high despite the plague years of the late seventeenth century: in the mid-1700s Naples had 369,000 inhabitants; ten years after the French Revolution, 441,000. Macaroni sustained this entire population, in spite of heavy taxation and the tyranny of Viceroy Molina and the Spanish viceregal regime.

In Silvio Fiorillo's comedy in the *commedia dell'arte* tradition, *La Lucilla costante* (1632), Pulcinella curses the rulers of Naples, crying out, "Ah spagnuolo, nemico delli maccarune!" (Oh you Spanish, enemies of macaroni).

The city was growing, and macaroni also provided a solution to urban expansion. Sereni states,

> Instead of transporting a watery and perishable foodstuff (*foglie*) from increasingly distant places and with noticeable expenditure, they transported a much richer dry commodity: grain. They used this to make an easily conserved product, transforming it *in loco* by adding water, which costs nothing, into an "alimentary mass": *pastasciutta* or pasta soup.

So extensive was this revolution that the "Neapolitan genius" of Naples's most popular figure adopted it as a full identity. One French traveler to Naples of the 1760s, Jérôme de Lalande, relates in his *Voyage en Italie* a witticism that made the rounds in those years: Pulcinella, "become king, responded in Neapolitan to someone who failed to give him macaroni because it was too common a dish, 'Mo mo me sprincepo'. (I resign my royalty right now.)"

Pulling the Mediterranean Bedclothes Toward the North

What occurred in Naples was an experiment in modernity. A major city readjusted its ability to survive by inventing a new alimentary tradition.

Italian Unity, just as startling a revolution, occurred at the same time. Once established, the new political entity of the Kingdom of Italy required a new and revolutionary image, identity, and customs if it was to share in the modernity of European nation states. Such a revolution was possible only by "pulling the Mediterranean bedclothes more to the north," and macaroni was an essential part of that operation. Between the eighteenth and nineteenth centuries, all of Northern Italy was facing a crisis of its own, arising from an erroneous interpretation of the abundance coming from the New World. Corn (maize) from the Americas had only partially resolved the problem of hunger in rural Northern Italy. Its sudden introduction was providential only in part, because it arrived without the gastronomic "know how" to make it a complete foodstuff. The Indios and *campesinos* of Aztec and Mayan lands who depended on corn knew that calcium must be added to corn flour to make it a complete foodstuff. Scholars and ethnobotanists such as Alfred

W. Crosby who study the biological revolution that resulted from the discovery of the New World wonder how maize could have arrived in Europe with no "recipe" for its treatment.

Montanari reminds us that

> Southern Italy would not witness the dramatic instances of malnutrition associated with dependence on maize or potatoes alone (potatoes were another importation from the New World). Thanks to the gluten of durum wheat—a coarser but more nutritious variety that grows only in the south—the peasants and poorer city-dwellers of southern Italy were better protected than their neighbors to the north.

Even in the South, however—as we have seen—pasta was not a daily dish until the eighteenth century. In order for pasta to become a national dish, something more was needed than just a convergence of technological and nutritional conditions and transformations. What made pasta begin to take hold lies in the symbolism with which it was invested, beginning with Cavour. Added to symbolism was the fact that the North took over the South, and the new nation needed a direct, simple, basic way to create customs common to all the inhabitants of the Peninsula.

Garibaldian Cuisine

It was, in fact, Garibaldi's stunning success in Sicily and the advance of his Thousand up the Italian Peninsula that enabled the culture of Northern Italy to establish contact with the population in the South. Massimo Alberini offers a vivid description of this phenomenon in his introduction to a collection of pasta and pizza recipes:

> Garibaldi's followers came mainly from areas where soup was served with rice, such as Bergamo and Piedmont. In fact, it was only a short time before the arrival of Garibaldi in Naples that the local *lazzari*, or street urchins, began eating macaroni or other pasta on anything like a regular basis. Even then it was rarely cooked at home: books by Delbono and the more colourful evidence of nineteenth-century lithographs by Dural, Ferdinando Palizzi and Duclère, as well as many anonymous watercolours of the Neapolitan school, show that it was common practice to buy a portion of pasta ready-cooked and mixed with cheese or tomato sauce from the nearest inn. Even the poorest Neapolitan enjoyed the human contact to be found in an inn, as well as his plate of *vermicelli* (little worms) and tomato sauce, or just *lattanti* (grated *pecorino* cheese).... So the Piedmontese, Lombards and Venetians who marched with Garibaldi made their first acquaintance with *vermicelli* and tomatoes.

They were joined several months later by regular regiments under Cialdini, dispersed to the South after the battle of Teano.

Camporesi concurs about the importance of Garibaldi's role in changing the Italian diet and, more generally, in the creation of "Italia Unita," a movement that was most obviously showcased in the Risorgimento's reconquest of the South.

Camporesi deals with the necessary topic of the tomato as well. Before about 1830, pasta was not served with tomato sauce. As an importation from the New World, tomatoes were regarded with diffidence. In fact, Ippolito Cavalcanti's *La Cucina casarinola co la lengua napolitana di Ippolito Cavalcanti duca di Buonvicino, appendice dialettale della cucina napoletana,* an early nineteenth-century cookbook written in dialect, does not list tomato sauce as an accompaniment for pasta, although it does list a simple tomato reduction to be used with fish, meat, fowl, or eggs. For this reason, Camporesi continues:

> Even more modern and revolutionary was Artusi's recognition of tomato sauce (rightly distinguished from simple tomato purée), which along with spaghetti was to be warmly accepted, not to say canonized, in the Italian culinary system. The new Artusian national cookery owed much to the triumphal entry of the tomato into what might be called Risorgimento cooking—or better still Garibaldian cooking, because after the March of the Thousand the tomato triumphantly spread through the whole peninsula. It gave new body and flavour to the eclectic, romantic cuisine, mainly brought in by the French, which survived in a tired form without originality or imagination even during the Restoration.

Camporesi introduces an incredible wealth of elements here, and he repeats (as he does at great length throughout this work) the comparison between the stately and rich cooking of the notables and the aristocracy of Northern Italy (a cuisine based on transalpine models) and the rowdy cuisine and substantially more robust Mediterranean foods firmly rooted in everyday life and domesticity. At this point pasta, at least symbolically, begins to unwind like a ball of yarn and wrap itself around the Italian identity.

Pasta (and Artusi) vs. Post-Unification Fragmentation

In his novel, *L'imperio*, Federico De Roberto depicts a dinner among Italian deputies to Parliament a few years after the unification of Italy. According to the description of Gian-Paolo Biasin in *I sapori della modernità*, as the delegates are eating their *vermicelli con le vongole* they

> heatedly debate the necessity of "unifying the Italian cuisines," or at least of "federating them," and they put forth "a national meal, an Italian dinner par excellence," but they agree only on starting off with a dish of macaroni, then dividing among "mullets Leghorn style, fried soles with calamari, beef stew with risotto, Modena *zampone* with spinach purée."

De Roberto's novel takes us back to an Italy that was fragmented even after unification, when pasta was generally accepted but everything else seemed still in flux. Camporesi states, citing the linguist Tullio De Mauro:

> The nation was divided by infinite regional peculiarities, patterns of customs and usages, weights and

measures, local traditions, popular oral cultures and parochialisms. For Italy, with its remote isolated and peripheral mountainous areas, its poor economic integration, the limited mobility of its workers and the circumscribed, rustic life of its people, national unity was a mythical and futuristic notion. It has been calculated that "in the years of national unification, speakers of Italian (as opposed to dialects)—far from representing all the citizens—numbered just over 600,000 in a total population of over 25 million people: in other words barely 2.5 per cent of the population. This is hardly more than the percentage designated in official statistics, then and later, as 'foreign language speakers.'"

We owe a debt of gratitude to Camporesi for his intuition of the importance of Pellegrino Artusi and his use of food to further the symbolic unity of the Italian people in the late nineteenth century. Someone was needed to synthesize and select from the many local and regional domestic cuisines: the creation of an "Italian" cuisine depended on the abstraction of genuine local cookery and the formation of a stereotype out of scattered bits and pieces.

Artusi's *La scienza in cucina e l'arte di mangiar bene* (Science in the kitchen and the art of eating well) was published in Florence in 1891. Artusi came from a middle-class merchant background; he was the son of a solidly established grocer in Forlimpopoli. *La scienza in cucina* sought to give a culinary homogeneity to Italy as a whole, moving out from the author's own dual linguistic and culinary background as a native of Romagna resident in Florence. Artusi went much farther afield than that, however, fusing elements from

Neapolitan and Sicilian cuisine into his work and making use of both old and new recipes. Above all, as Camporesi points out, "the witty, amiable little Tuscan-Romagnol book by the good-natured banker in Piazza d'Azeglia... insinuated itself into a great many homes in all the regions of Italy," and it did so by rejecting both overly humble and overly sumptuous dishes and by adjusting spicier tastes and richer ingredients to an acceptable mid-level.

The work met with extraordinary success, and with every new edition Artusi hastened to add to and correct, not only the recipes themselves, but the dialectical elements in the Italian used in the text to describe them.

Artusi's work responded to the demands of a growing public—the new Italian middle class—that was eager to free itself, in its cuisine as well as in other areas, from models from north of the Alps that had been the standard for high cuisine. That middle class dreamed of a "middling" self-image such as the one projected by Luigi Arnaldo Vassallo ("Gandoin") in *La Famiglia De Tappetti*, one of the first works of Italian fiction to depict everyday bourgeois life—that is, an image in harmony with the modest and tranquil values of a new class of clerks and housewives. Camporesi says of *La scienza in cucina*:

> The book's success is best explained by the fact that Artusi came on the scene at the opportune moment, in a period of transition when Italian cooking was tired and decadent—narrowly regional on the one hand, French on the other (the menus of courts and official banquets, even at the

municipal level, were French in form and substance). The book's purism and its linguistic and culinary patriotism filled a great void in the Italian national consciousness, which in those same years was reviving old rancours and hostilities towards "our not-so-benevolent neighbours," the French.

Camporesi was not exaggerating. Artusi did indeed succeed in doing what it is not sure that Manzoni accomplished:

> It must be recognized that *La scienza in cucina* did more for national unification than Manzoni's great novel, *I promessi sposi* (The Betrothed). Artusi's gustatory principles created a code of national identification, where Manzoni's linguistic and stylistic principles failed.

Artusi's attempt to simplify Italian regional cooking in the aim of inventing a "national character" were lodged within a change that lucid minds had been aware of from the earliest years of the movement for national unification.

Up to then, the Sicilian aristocracy had lived until then calling French cooks "monsù."[4]

---

[4]T. Spadaccino, the editor of *La Sicilia dei Marchesi e del Monsù*, speaks of a cookbook written by Grazietta Tedeschi, marchesa of Modica, prefacing his remarks with an anecdote showing that in patrician families only the cook, *il monsù*, had the right to reject criticism from the lady of the house. *Il monsù* had prepared a dish of pasta with sardines, to which he had added tomato sauce, a combination that shocked the marchesa. When she remonstrated, he replied that this was the custom in other patrician houses, an observation that reduced the lady of the house to silence.

In Giuseppe Tomasi di Lampedusa's *Il Gattopardo* (The Leopard), the Prince of Salina decides to serve his guests, notables of the town of Donnafugata, a dish of baked maccaroni. Don Fabrizio is quite aware of the changes that are occurring throughout the Peninsula (even though he accepts his nephew Tancredi's statement, "If we want things to stay as they are, things will have to change"), and he has no hesitation about breaking rules: "The Prince was too experienced to offer Sicilian guests, in a town of the interior, a dinner beginning with soup, and he infringed the rules of *haute cuisine* all the more readily as he disliked it himself."

The *pasticcio di maccheroni* that the monsù prepared for the prince and his guests was, however, a further example of synthesis between high cuisine and the arrival of more prosaic cooking. Artusi, as Gian-Paolo Biasin notes, includes a similar dish in his *Scienza* under the title, *pasticcio di maccheroni*, stating that the dish is *all'uso di Romagna*. The baked pasta dish that Tomasi di Lampedusa describes is much more luxurious, however:

> The burnished gold of the crusts, the fragrance of sugar and cinnamon they exuded, were but preludes to the delights released from the interior when the knife broke the crust; first came a smoke laden with aromas, then chicken livers, hard-boiled eggs, sliced ham, chicken, and truffles in masses of piping-hot, glistening macaroni, to which the meat juice gave an exquisite hue of suède.

Praise and Disparagement:
From the Duke of Salaparuta to Leopardi

Artusi's book also met with success because it accompanied the emergence of an ideology of foods that were "Italian," "healthy," patriotic, and simple, the essence of which, the *nec plus ultra* and the banner, was pasta.

The "Italian" style and the reminder that Italians were brava gente found a completely new elaboration thanks to *pastasciutta* in very different circles ranging from Sicilian aristocrats pursuing better heath through vegetarian cuisine and embracing diet reform as if it were a mission to supporters of patriotic and irredentist fanfares.

One such enthusiast was the Duke of Salaparuta, who launched Corvo wine, a red Sicilian wine, in 1824. He states:

> Observe, for example, all the peasants of Sicily, whose daily diet is pasta dressed only with olive oil, cheese, or tomato, without the addition or accompaniment of meat or animal fats. They are reserved in temperament, have great inner strength, and are resistant to the heaviest labors under the lash of the summer sun or winter's rigors. They do not even know what obesity is, or laziness or corpulence, whereas the moment we raise our eyes to the more well-to-do classes, where the first luxury that people indulge in is to add to their pasta sausage, ground meat, clams, and animal fats, we immediately see laziness, obesity, along with serious consequence that appear in their organisms.

Not only peasants, but soldiers, undaunted Alpine troops, and Bersaglieri enter the picture. In the words of Paolo Monelli (as quoted by Luigi Sada), an interventionist who supported Italy's entry into World War I as a return to the true Italian character:

> I know not how the neutralists, the reformers, and the shirkers from military service feed their soft stomachs, their adipose reasons for reform, their varicose veins, and their myopia, but I am persuaded that for four years now the infantry soldiers of Italy have found in *pastasciutta* the leaven for their hero- ism and tenacity and sustenance for their muscles as they fly over Monte Santo, climb up the Tofane group, slide on the glaciers, tumble down slopes to the reconquered areas, and swim across the Piave.... A mess tin brimming with rigatoni and a cup of brisk red wine, what joy for the common soldier returning from a week of dried rations and snow- melt! And how reconciled he feels to his harsh profession and his disappointments! *Pastasciutta* also nourished the trim alacrity of the Arditi, the sharp watch of the sailors on torpedo boats, the focused senses of the airplane pilots.

For similar reasons but with a quite different inspiration, the Futurist Filippo Tommaso Marinetti has this to say: "Pastaciutta, however agreeable to the palate, is a passéist food because it makes people heavy, brutish, deludes them into thinking it is nutritious, makes them skeptical, slow, pessimistic." *The Manifesto of Futurist Cooking*, published in the *Gazetta del Popolo* of Turin on 28 December 1930, states:

Convinced that in the probable future conflagration those who are most agile, most ready for action, will win, we Futurists... [a]bove all... believe necessary: a) The abolition of pastasciutta, an absurd Italian gastronomic religion. It may be that a diet of cod, roast beef, and steamed pudding is beneficial to the English; cold cuts and cheese to the Dutch and sauerkraut, smoked [salt] pork and sausage to the Germans, but pasta is not beneficial to the Italians. For example it is completely hostile to the vivacious spirit and passionate, generous, intuitive soul of the Neapolitans. If these people have been heroic fighters, inspired artists, awe-inspiring orators, shrewd lawyers, tenacious farmers it was in spite of their voluminous daily plate of pasta. When they eat it they develop that typical ironic and sentimental scepticism which can often cut short their enthusiasm. An extremely intelligent Neapolitan professor, Signorelli, writes, "In contrast to bread and rice, pasta is a food which is swallowed, not masticated. Such starchy food should mainly be digested in the mouth by the saliva but in this case the task of transformation is carried out by the pancreas and the liver. This leads to an interrupted equilibrium in these organs. From such disturbances derive lassitude, pessimism, nostalgic inactivity and neutralism."

Marinetti could say all this, however, because pasta had already become symbolic for the Italian people. Despite their inverted perspective, the Futurists felt obligated to start off from a solid national base. Still, it seems odd that one could be non-interventionist by eating (or not eating) spaghetti.

Before Marinetti, Giacomo Leopardi offered in his *Zibaldone* arguments against *pastasciutta* that were not only more cogent but also, Giuseppe Prezzolini tells us, more personal.

Leopardi did not like spaghetti because, as a solitary eater, he thought it encouraged *compotazione* —eating in company—and he preferred silent mastication to the reprehensible habit of talking while eating. Leopardi understood the ineluctably social nature of a plate of spaghetti. For that reason, he preferred tiny soup pasta, a more discreet and solitary form. Even he, however, was going against the grain in a situation in which, by that time, spaghetti was fast becoming the norm.

The Taganrog Story

There were also technical reasons for the success of dried pasta. Thanks to a revolution in alimentary production, it was a modern commodity. The causes of that modernization were connected with the transformation of Italy into a unified market, however.

This meant that the durum wheat that Vespasian first imported from the Chersonesus (the Crimean Peninsula), which the Romans called *triticum* and used to grind into flour called *simila*, became an important commodity. Ships that sailed the Mediterranean with full cargoes were unloaded in Genoa and Naples. The grain, *triticum durum* (as distinct from *triticum vulgare*) may have originated in Afghanistan, and in the ancient world it had been cultivated in Syria and Palestine. Its advantage was that it had a genetic makeup different from other grains (twenty-eight chromosomes rather than forty-two) and was richer in gluten—that is, it was endowed with a higher proportion of proteins that made it more able to absorb water and withstand cooking.

The same Crimean grain contributed to one of the many memorable moments of the Risorgimento, if we can believe one of the major pasta manufacturers of Italy, Vincenzo Agnesi.

It was 1883, and a Ligurian sailor, Giovanni B. Cuneo, notified of his probable arrest as a Mazzini supporter, hurried to board a ship. After his arrival in Taganrog, he was discoursing in an inn about the unhappy conditions in Italy (at the time subjugated and divided), seeking to dazzle his dubious listeners, sailors from all over Italy, with the promise of a better future. At that point a blond young man appeared in the back of the room, listened attentively to the speaker, and then ran up to embrace him. The occasion was perfect for enrolling him in Giovane Italia. You might almost say that thanks to spaghetti and its irreplaceable prime ingredient, Taganrog was the start of Garibaldi's great adventure in pursuit of the mirage of a unified Italy.

Durum wheat became the hero of national unity as well as representing a myth worthy of a spy story for pasta manufacturers like Vincenzo Agnesi and his sons and nephews.

In fact, as Agnesi declares, Ligurian and Neapolitan pasta makers held Taganrog wheat to be indispensable. Their local durum wheat just did not have the same proportion of gluten or the same remarkable characteristics. Pasta made with Taganrog wheat had a color, a consistency, and nutritive qualities that were unbeatable and even unrivaled. This was true to the point that wheat from the Crimean Peninsula evaded trade protections. Agnesi continues:

> The Bourbon kingdom was essentially agricultural, as stated in the *Penny Magazine of Useful Knowledge* of 1830, and the importation of foreign wheat was discouraged. The pasta manufacturers, however, had always claimed that they were unable to produce good macaroni without the grain that came from Russia and, precisely, from the port of Taganrog, a city situated in the northernmost point of the Sea of Azov. Given that any decline in the quality of the national dish was considered a genuine calamity, the importation [of Russian wheat] continued to be permitted, even though growers in the Kingdom of Naples often found no market for the wheat that they produced.

Taganrog did indeed provide the best durum wheat. The resulting dough was not very elastic or extensible, but it was resistant and, since it was more inclined to tear than stretch, good for shorter shapes. Taganrog wheat contained no less that 17% gluten, dried, and approximately 20% total nitrogen. The latter mattered less than the quality of the gluten, which is what counts most in pasta making. When the Russian Revolution broke out in 1917, the Crimea went through terrible times, with the result that in Taganrog and elsewhere wheat was no longer exported, but rather consumed by a famished population, to the point that it became extinct. From that time on, the myth of Taganrog obsessed Italian pasta manufacturers, who attempted in vain to seek out the cultivar at the source. It seems that Italy lost not only the nutritive qualities of Taganrog wheat, but also a savor that modern-day Italians can only imagine. Talking over dinner some time ago with the heir to the Soresi pasta manufactory in Sicily, I asked him what Taganrog pasta might have tasted like and what our ancestors, should they return to this world, might say about the flavor of the pasta that we eat today. Leonardo Soresi replied that our tastes have probably changed along with the taste of our pasta. It is in fact true that what we eat today may not be made from Taganrog wheat, but our pasta has also not been dried slowly or been drawn out in the old manner. Slow drying led to a slight fermentation that gave the pasta a hint of acidity, and the old extrusion process created pores that enabled the pasta to absorb a greater quantity of sauce.

Success: Technical Conditions from Torre del Greco to Genoa

That said, we can pass on to more strictly technical aspects that will help to understand how a desire to spread the use of a national foodstuff came about.

Processing pasta is a complicated matter, and we know from documents of the various trade associations involved that there were many trade secrets. The Statutes of the Arte dei fidalaeri—the *fedelini* makers' guild—drawn up in Genoa in 1538, provides one example of such a document. We have even earlier evidence: master lasagna-makers sailed on board the galleys of Paganin Doria in the fourteenth century. Moreover, trade associations tended to gather on the same street, as the pasta-makers did in Palermo on the Ruga dei Maccherunari alla Kalsa, as evidenced in a notarial act from Palermo dated 5 August 1447.

Massimo Alberini summarizes the three stages of pasta-making:

> In the first stage the flour and water were mixed. Secondly, the dough was put in a kneader; in the South three or more men operated a sort of bar to rotate it, whereas in Liguria it was done with a wheel rotating in a wooden trough. When the dough was smooth and compact it went through a third stage, by which a mechanical press (*l'ingegno*, or "gadget," invented by the Neapolitans) with a screw plunger pressed the pasta down on to a perforated copper disc, the die-plate, which could be changed to make spaghetti, macaroni, *rigatoni* or other similar shapes, and a revolving knife then controlled the length of the pasta as it came through the die-plate (short pasta was made when the knife worked extra fast). The pasta was next laid across canes hooked on to a wooden frame to dry. The frame was put out on a terrace or over the street in southern Italy, or propped up against more canes in a well ventilated room in Liguria. Pasta-making was by no means easy; each stage required careful supervision…. [Aside from the guilds,] [v]arious other exclusive academies and universities of *vermicelli-* and *lasagne*-makers exercised a rigid control over the whole industry.

As early as 1789 the Kingdom of Naples was exporting manufactured pasta for a total cost of some 176,000 ducats, and it was in Naples that Thomas Jefferson bought the machine that he had shipped back to the United States in order to introduce macaroni to his compatriots. In 1787, two years before the outbreak of the French Revolution, Paul Jacques Malouin published an *Art du vermicelier* with the aim of encouraging the importation of Neapolitan pasta-making techniques, and French contact with Italy in the wars under the Directory and the Empire increased French consumption of pasta. Between 1820 and 1840 macaroni became the rage in France, and Balzac was extremely fond of the dish, as Jean-Paul Aron reminds us.

Modern industrially produced pasta was launched in Italy during the latter half of the nineteenth century thanks to two innovations that Garibaldian propaganda had made technologically possible. The first was a *semolatrice* or motorized sieve, a machine invented in Marseille and adopted in Naples in 1878 that made it possible to sift out fine select-grade semolina more efficiently than with a hand sieve. The workers in Torre Annunziata, a town whose economy was based on pasta production, rioted and burned the Marseilles "starvation machines." Troops were called out, and fifty of the workers were sentenced to from two to six years in prison.

In 1882 C. and T. T. Pattison, an English firm that had an iron works in Naples, produced new mechanical mixers, knife-equipped kneading machines, and mechanized pasta presses. (The first cylindrical mills had already been introduced.) Employment picked up, though on a different basis. In Torre Annunziata fifty-four pasta works gave jobs to ten thousand workers, and employment rose in Torre del Greco, Gragnano, Portici, and Castellammare as well.

Genoa pasta was yellow, thanks to the addition of saffron, but the Neapolitan firms produced a translucent, amber-colored pasta (thus displaying a remaining nostalgia for Taganrog) that was esteemed "both for the air and for the water," as was said at the time, because the dough was thinned with boiling water and then quickly dried in the sun. Naples's domination of pasta manufacturing lasted some fifty years, and part of the industry's success was due to demand among emigrants to the Americas, as we shall see in the next chapter.

Paolo Agnesi traveled from Genoa to Naples toward the end of the nineteenth century to study the great industrial success of Neapolitan pasta. His observations on this trip changed both pasta production and the market for the finished product—to his advantage. His sons shifted from hydraulic presses to continuous presses; even more important, they had the genial idea of packaging the finished product. Up to then, pasta had been sold in bulk, and the shopkeeper's word was the only guarantee of its quality. Not only did the Agnesi firm invent standardized packaging, they also began to put cooking instructions and advertizing material on their packages.

This brings us to the threshold of another great transformation. Italian-made pasta went abroad, where it created an even more pronounced Italianness, a reverse image, "seen from the outside," of what Italians are like, how they talk, gesticulate, and behave, and how they differ from the non-Italians around them.

But What About Pizza?

Obviously, pizza has always existed, and not just on the Italian Peninsula. Flattening a ball of flour mixed with water and cooking it on a hot slab, in a metal pan, or inside an oven is a primitive activity that goes back to the origins of humankind. All it takes is a grain or a compact substance that can be ground into flour and a source of heat. Mexican tortillas made of ground corn and the flat rice cakes of many Oriental peoples all require the same basic movements of a hand that mixes the dough, compacts it, and pats it down on a smooth surface. Food in a circular shape, like the sun or the moon, may be as old as the wheel.

Where wheat is concerned (the grain that interests us here), the acts of mixing, spreading out, and putting the dough to cook, either by direct contact or in an oven, can be traced throughout the ancient Mediterranean world and the Middle East as far as India.

Even today there are impressive resemblances in flat breads, ranging from the pita bread of the Arab world (a thin, unleavened round that is often split and filled with mutton—*schwarma*—or chick peas and garlic—*felafel*) to the Indian *nan* (which resembles a plain pizza filled with condiments and cooked in a tandoori oven), or, in the Slavic tradition, *blinis* (lightly leavened fried bread), and the genuine *pizze* and *pizzette* of the Turkish tradition. All of these reflect a common intuition: a flat base or pocket to be enriched with a modest or elaborate topping or filling.

Eating the Table and Re-Mixing the World

When cooked, the flat wheat mix serves as a support for meat, fish, or vegetables; as a tablecloth; or as an edible plate. Ethiopians still repeat the rite of setting a table with soft, thin sheets of a bread product that serves simultaneously as a dipper to eat with, a tablecloth, and a basic food.

In all of these various forms, pizza-like breads respond to an immediate need: they are at once utensil, a place on which to put food, and itself a food. They permit the consumption of sauces, dips, small mouthfuls, olives, and spices with no need for any implement besides one's hands. Bread, focaccia or any flat form permits moving about or from one place to another, and encourages offering and sharing broken-off pieces. The base can be pliant, like Italian pizza or Indian *nan*; or it can be rigid, like the Berber bread of Algeria, Sardinian "music paper," or the *piadina* of Romagna. Rigid forms have the added fascination of a compact, homogeneous product that lasts longer and gives us the impression that we are eating a resistant surface; they are an object more than a food.

Neapolitan pizza is the reduction to a stereotype of thousands of flat breads: *pinze, sfincioni, sfincionelli, schiacciate, focacce, crescie, crescenti, puddiche, pitte, impanate, farinate, calzoni, bruschette, moffolette,* and *pani cunzati,* leaving aside the thousands of local terms for forms still current in the fragmented world of Italian breads, leavened and unleavened. The very controversy over the etymology of the term "pizza" indicates the food's great age. Some derive the term from the Greek *plàx,* a flat or flattened surface. In the Roman world the vendors of flat bread were called *placentarii.* Others think that "pizza" derives from *pinsa,* a noun form taken from the Latin verb *pinsere* (and the analogous *pistare,* to crush, grind, reduce to mush or pulp), and in fact bakers were called *pistores* and *pistus* was the soft dough common to bread and foccacia.

As is evident, the verbs that provide the nouns in the constellation of terms relating to the various forms of pasta and pizza occupy more or less the same semantic area in Latin and Italian, as is true of *maccare/ammaccare; pistare/impasto.* Italian alimentary culture requires breaking up something hard and recomposing it by working it into a malleable mass. If the original matter is to become edible, it must be reduced to powder and mixed with water, as if it were clay.

The gesture of providing food should closely reflect the gesture of the Creator and Creation. Only those capable of remodeling the world are permitted to nourish themselves. Extraordinarily, breaking down their foods is a ritual common to cultures very distant from each other. In Papua New Guinea, in Polynesia, and in certain parts of Africa, for example, manioc root, taro root, and tree cores cannot be eaten as they are harvested, but must be reduced to pulp and recomposed, shaped within leaf containers made for the purpose. To eat is a way of questioning the form in which the world is presented to us and to propose other, more human forms. There must be distance between the available resources—the fruits of the earth, game—and the mouth, which is a cultural place, hence is charged with not accepting the world as it is. Among the Achuar of the Ecuadoran back country, "God's gifts" in the form of raw bananas and *toronjas* (an immense, grapefruit-like fruit) are insufficient to feed a man. The men will let themselves die of starvation if raw foodstuffs are not worked by the hands and, in particular, the mouths of the women of the tribe, who chew plant products, turning them into a fermented mush for consumption by the village.

From Powder into the Flames

In pizza this ancient transformation of a solid substance into powder and form is recent, evident, and traceable. The round that we eat recalls the proximity of that time-honored material and the immediacy of the flame lit to transform it. One of the strongest deterrents to the McDonaldization of pizza is that seeing the oven is an essential part of this return to the original transformation of matter.

The ancient Hindu god of fire, Agni, was adored in the form of an altar of baked bricks with a flame shooting up from it. The god was both the fire and the altar. In the modern food industry, the wood-fired pizza oven is all that remains to remind us of the original alimentary gesture and the sacrificial nature of matter.

The oven consecrates the dough that is placed in it, transforming it into something accessible for human consumption, a food that arises out of fire, stone, water, and pulverized wheat.

There are indications that expert *pizzaioli*—pizza-makers—are among the most sought-after and best-paid members of the restaurant trade. Recent estimates tell us that the immediate need for manpower in this field is something like ten thousand persons. Skilled *pizzaioli* can choose between full-time, part-time, or occasional or seasonal work, not only in Italy but in the United States, Germany, Iceland, and even in the Far East, Japan, and Malaysia, with stipends than can reach 3,000,000 lire (or, in more recent times, 3,500 euros) a month, even $5,000 in far-off places such as Latvia.

The *pizzaiolo* maintains the air of priestly keeper of the flame that today's chefs have lost. Not only is he not closed up inside the kitchen; his visibility is one of the restaurant's attractions.

He provides a unique spectacle: the mounds of dough, the smack of his palms and thumbs as he flattens one, flying arms as he forms a disk, his light touch as his fingers and eyes control the quantity of the ingredients, the fistful of flour he throws onto the peel, and his warrior's thrust as he brings the shiny white round of dough to rest near the mouth of the oven, knowing that its first contact with heat is the most important one. No one is more respected than the pizzaiolo as he waits, seeming to do nothing, as the transformation takes place inside the oven, where branches, logs, and hot coals, the whitened oven ceiling, smoke, creaks, crackles, and perfumed gusts tell him—and only him—when the precise moment has come to fetch out food for humans.

Neapolitan Pizza "Laboratories"

The question of pizza, first as a Neapolitan invention, then as an Italian invention, is much less important than one might think. I see the invention of pizza as a return to and a crystallization of an archetypical form of something typical, historical, and local. Admittedly, in Naples the flat bread of Virgil's peasants or the *picia* that Horace mentions—even the *piza* attested in the medieval Latin of Gaeta in 997—becomes an urban food for the common people.

The earliest recorded pizza establishments in Naples appeared between the late seventeenth and the early eighteenth centuries as "laboratories" where dough was worked and cooked and passers-by could buy a pizza.

We know from Gabriele Benincasa that Dorotea di Capua, the marchesa di Campolattaro, a "most beautiful, [but] equally capricious woman," knowing that her pregnant condition would win her indulgence and sure of her influence over the viceroy, Don Pietro Giron, duca d'Ossuna, expressed a desire for a pizza during a ball at Court, a whim that was immediately gratified. This passing fancy was aristocratic, but it shows proof of a certain *frisson*, a thrill connected with the plebeian.

Still in Naples, a pizzeria named "Zi' Ciccio" can be documented on Piazza Cavour as early as 1727. On the Salita di Santa Teresa in 1732 there was the pizzeria "Ntuono" that Ferdinando I, the king of the Two Sicilies, liked to visit incognito (another case of "royal" thrills and plebeian tastes). Benincasa, who is Neapolitan of origin, tells us that the pizzeria "Port'Alba" opened in 1738 near the city gate of that name, and that it "is still there." In 1748 another pizzeria opened on Spaccanapoli; in 1750 the pizzeria "Capasso" opened near Porta San Gennaro; and in 1760 we have word of the pizzeria "Da Pietro" (later "Brandi"), whose fortunes came to be connected with the new royal house of Italy and the invention of pizza margherita. Royal and aristocratic escapes into plebeian realms paid their democratic dues when pizza was given formal status at court.

Pizza and the Flag

In the early eighteenth century pizzerias were indeed apt to be "laboratories," places with a bake oven to which one went but where one did not linger. Only in the mid-century did twenty of the eighty pizza shops in Naples open an area for the consumption of pizza *in loco*, thanks to little marble tables attached to the wall, Benincasa tells us, "so they would not be carried off."

Consumed at a table in this manner, pizza lost its original connotation, documented by many foreign travelers and contemporary prints, of being a food bought from an ambulant seller and eaten on the street, although until recent times pizza shops continued to serve customers on foot and refurnish the ambulant pizza sellers. Until the 1850s, the latter continued to ply the streets of Naples with a *stufa* on their heads—a circular copper and brass container with shelves of perforated metal that kept the pizza hot. It was undoubtedly one of those *stufe* that provided the pizza enjoyed by Alexandre Dumas, the author of *The Three Musketeers*, who arrived in Naples in 1835. He writes in his travel memoir, *Le Corricolo*,

> It is a sort of flat bread, like those made at Saint-Denis; it is round in form and is worked with the same dough as bread. At first view it is a simple dish: after examination, it will seem more complicated... Pizza can be had with oil, with bacon, with lard, with cheese, with tomatoes, and with small fish. It is the gastronomic thermometer of the market: its price rises or falls according to the cost of the above-mentioned ingredients and their freshness.

Dumas also documents the fact that pizza could be had "ogge a otto"—literally, payable within eight days. This variety was fried, and for the most part it was made at improvised cook stands within the courtyard doors of private dwellings. In reality, this sort of pizza establishment seems to have been a clandestine set-up for lending money at usurious rates. In a story set in the Fondaco Pozillo, one of the poorest streets in Naples, Salvatore Di Giacomo speaks of pizza as a popular dish, a resource for the hungry and the poorest city-dwellers.

He describes one family that had made an agreement for "a subscription with the neighborhood pizza-maker, so that for four pennies a day he would set aside [for them] all the uneaten pizza crusts" accumulated through the day.

When Di Giacomo was writing for the *Corriere di Napoli* the Italian Unity movement was in full bloom. Pizza was still a poor man's dish, but in four years it had risen to the rank of a patriotic and "Risorgimental" dish, thanks to a certificate that the royal house had conceded to the *pizzaiolo* Raffaele Esposito to use the name *margherita* for the pizza with basil, mozzarella cheese, and tomato made in honor of Queen Margherita. The official historians of pizza insist that the document does not refer to the invention of "*pizza margherita*" but only to the use of the name. Surely a pizza with those ingredients already existed and had been eaten by the Bourbon royals, openly or incognito, along with many other Neapolitans.

What happened in June 1889 had more far-reaching consequences. A messenger of the royal house of Savoy invited Raffaele Esposito, the owner of the pizzeria "Pietro... e basta così" located in the Salita Sant'Anna di Palazzo to come cook at the court.

History tells us that Queen Margherita had expressed a desire to break the monotony of French cooking. The pizza-maker and his wife went to Capodimonte in a small wagon pulled by a mule, bringing along all the ingredients necessary for the preparation of pizza. Capodimonte already possessed a pizza oven because Ferdinando II, the Bourbon king, in imitation of his grandfather Ferdinando I (the one who used to go incognito to the pizzeria Ntuono) asked Ntuono's son to construct a brick oven there big enough to bake seven pizzas at once.

The documents tell us that Raffaele Esposito used the old régime's oven to make three pizzas. Tradition has it that in order to avoid garlic, considered inappropriate for female royalty, he eliminated *pizza alle marinara*, which meant that his choice was restricted to a *pizza bianca* (with oil, cheese, and basil), one with *cecenielle* (little fish), and one with a red, white, and green topping of tomato, mozzarella, and basil. Here tradition diverges: either the latter was a politically motivated, last-minute inspiration using the colors of the Italian flag and named for the queen, or else an already familiar pizza with a topping of mozzarella, tomato, and basil suddenly found a new name, meaning, and historical function.

Whether either version of this story is true or not, it is an extraordinary example of the invention of a tradition, because it contains all the elements of a redefinition of a viewpoint. We find in it the populism typical of a new monarchy, but with the additional and ultra-modern imprint of a new capacity for using symbols and myths and for "pulling the bedclothes of the Mediterranean to the north" that we have already seen in the context of pasta. It also reflects a detachment from France and from anti-Risorgimento Europe. The queen's statement about the "monotony" of French cooking shows her as a northern woman, unaware of how varied and joyous life in the South could be, and it shows that pizza, by itself, could represent that vitality.

In the nationalist and populist soul of the Risorgimento there is yet another element, which is that of taking possession of another people's history by changing its signs. Ferdinando's oven demonstrates that the Bourbon monarchs had always been aware of and enjoyed the southern character of Naples. The new rulers from Savoy, thousands of kilometers to the north, took over from the preceding crowned heads and imitating their rituals to the point that people forgot that such rituals had been devised by others.

We know just what Don Fabrizio, in *The Leopard*, would have said to the emissary from the Turin government, come to ask him to be senator of the Kingdom of Sardinia: "My dear Chevalley, if we want things to stay as they are, things will have to change." But here he (and Tancredi) would have been wrong. It was precisely the strategy of the image that underlay Italian Unity, that found its most genial instrument in food, and that made it possible for modernity to make its entry with pasta and pizza, passed off as the reinvention of popular tradition.

II
Pasta and Pizza in the World: The Great Emigration

Emigration from Italy belongs among the extraordinary movements of mankind. In its chief lineaments it has no like. Through the number of men it has involved and the course it has pursued, through its long continuance on a great scale and its role in other lands, it stands alone.

—Robert F. Foerster,
The Italian Emigration of Our Times

In Chapter 1 we have seen how "Italianness" was constructed in Italy through a complex process in which Northern Italy adopted a more Mediterranean cast that had come to be valued as part of the national identity. Genoa, Naples, and Sicily were the focus of a reinvented tradition also based in a new and strong need for individuation. The new kingdom strove to create a degree of homogeneity, to which Artusi's cookbook, military service, the schools, television, and pasta all contributed. In part, that homogeneity had already been achieved because Italy was a land of wheat eaters. What changed is that durum wheat came to be used for a product that could be industrially mass-produced, then packaged, exported, and distributed elsewhere. That process, which took place within Italy from the 1870s to the end of the century, soon coincided with the sweeping emigration of Italians to other lands.

Whatever the nature and complexity of the causes of that diaspora, it is hardly fortuitous that a mass movement of the sort took place after the realization of a unified Italy. The South was becoming increasingly poor in comparison to the North; customary law was abrogated and feudal lands expropriated by the new unified state; heavy taxes made survival impossible in a peasant world that until then had held together thanks to the laxity of the "pre-modern" system of the Bourbon rulers.

A mass exodus struck the South as the entire peasant world was turned upside down in the restructuring of the Peninsula. Unified Italy became a land of massive emigration; leading the list of nations of emigrants at the end of the nineteenth century. When these "recent" Italian citizens, who spoke a number of languages and dialects, crossed the ocean, they were asked, "Who are you?"

Their response to that question depended on an identity that was still fluid, but that could be defined by their touchiness, by external signs, and by how they gathered together as a group.

Their "external face" reflected ways of being that newly forged Italians were just becoming aware of. "Italianness" was a particular sort of domesticity. Pasta (spaghetti in particular) and pizza were an integral part of that external image. Thus similar problems faced those abroad and those at home. Abroad the problem for Italians was to present an appealing image of Italianness as a means of defense; at home it was to fit in with an increasing homogeneity. Both at home and abroad, the history of pasta after Italian unification is one of the incessant elaborations of a *koinè* that was alimentary even before it was linguistic.

Moreover, that *koinè* was focused on a certain way of living, of keeping a house and maintaining a household, derived from Italian civic tradition and from a habit of living in a small town, village, or isolated center with a pretense of urbanity and a tradition of a strong domesticity.

In the early twentieth century (from 1901 to 1913), 91 percent of Italian immigrants to the United States came from Southern Italy. That flood of Italians was made up of people of peasant background, but who had become accustomed to living in a big center with access to country areas reachable on foot or by muleback. Tight-knit groups of this sort of folk arrived in New York, Boston, or San Francisco, where they a created a strong community, a "Little Italy" with its own highly visible characteristics.

"Made in Italy" Before the Fact

If there is one characteristic that stands out in the world's view of Italy in the decades after Italian unification, it is precisely this talent for creating a *paese*—a world in which the private domain invades public space in the form of potted plants placed in front of the houses, laundry drying in Mulberry Street courtyards, fruit sold from pushcarts or carefully arranged outside a store—plus a tendency to extroversion rather than defense, to preferring the public stage over privacy. The very notion of "privacy" even seems absurd when applied to a culture in which the private was to some extent already public, in the sense that it was an elaboration of the public scene brought into the home.

This is why the Italian quarter on Manhattan's Lower East Side seemed a large outdoor market, a stage on which a life lived outside the house was expressed with an exaggeration in which even miserable poverty played a role. If we fail to grasp the strong pull of domesticity, we will never understand how it became the "brand name" of Italianness; the secret of success (as the epigraph to this chapter reminds us) of Italians abroad. Pasta was not only a brilliant economic invention but also the logo and the banner of this "globalization" of the image of Italy.

Unlike other sizable immigrant groups—the Irish, for instance, who were held together by their Catholicism, or the Jews, a compact group thanks to religious endogamy—the religion of Italians abroad became domesticity: *la casa*. That same penchant for domesticity helps us to understand Italians' involvement in criminality in their new land. The house—*la casa*—became the public sign of Italianness, whether Italians were targets of laughter or examples of the glory or the cleverness of selling a wretchedly provincial small world as universal. Was the later and hard-won success of "Made in Italy" anything else but an ability to sell a micro-familiar "humility" or arrogance? Of an ability to sell the house itself, the genius for creating a *casa* open to universal imitation? Later, Martin Scorsese, Al Pacino, and Robert De Niro offered archetypes of an Italianness made of toughness and generous sentiments, street poverty and a family-style welcome.

Who invented all this? Did it emerge from the desperation of the first Italians to arrive in America, or from the cleverness of a fortunate few like the pasta manufacturer, Caruso? However it came about, the ability to sell the terribly local as universal was unique. This success resembles the magic of a chemical or physical transformation, the seeming miracle of an extremely compact mass passing from the solid state to a gas.

Pasta and pizza played a major role in this process. Pasta is an elaboration of one kind of home cooking—*la cucina della mamma*—and in America it created a boom in home-style Italian restaurants. Pizza reflects the revolution of eating out inexpensively. It is the invention of a "carry-out" food of a highly inventive frugality in the almost archaeological form of a flat round baked dough made from leavened bread flour and water to which simple toppings such as tomato, onion, and cheese can be added, both for decoration and taste. Pasta, on the other hand, requires knowing how to cook it, preparing a sauce, and eating it in a home atmosphere.

Emigration and the emigrants were responsible for spreading the image of Italians throughout the world. Spaghetti and other sorts of pasta, along with pizza, have become synonymous with Italianness, in the dual sense that they provided an image of Italy to be presented to non-Italians, and did so well before a parallel process took place in their homeland.

In his introduction to Pellegrino Artusi's *La scienza in cucina*, Piero Camporesi sketches a magnificent fresco of the contribution of foodstuffs to defining an Italian identity after Italian unification. What he neglects to mention is that such an operation would never have succeeded (at least, not in the same terms) without the twenty-six million Italian emigrants who crossed the ocean during the century that followed the unification of Italy.

Pasta, Like Coca-Cola

As early as 1880, Torre Annunziata, with its fifty-four pasta manufacturers, produced pasta and shipped it in the holds of the Rubattino and Lloyd Sabaudo line ships. Massimo Alberini tells us that the wharfs were stacked high with heavy boxes lined with resistant blue paper containing twenty-five or fifty kilos of macaroni and long spaghetti in five-kilo packages bearing the label "Napoli Bella Brand" and "Vesuvio Brand."

In 1900 the De Cecco firm instituted an artificial drying process that enabled its pasta products to withstand shipment from Abruzzo to Naples and on to New York, and for the American market it added vitamins to its products.

Tomatoes were also made accessible on a broad scale by the American businessman William Underwood, who, as early as 1835, imported seeds from England and began to can tomatoes for domestic use and European export.

As Jack Goody notes, it was the Italian immigrants of the first decades of the twentieth century who both spread the use of pasta products and were their prime target market. The widespread consumption of pasta (and pizza) in America, a genuine stimulus to its success throughout the world, is comparable to that of another universal product: Coca-Cola.

Coca-Cola became America's national symbol during World War II. It was a perfect carrier for family and cultural memories for the thousands of Americans serving in the armed forces throughout the world, who not only enjoyed drinking Coke, but might even write home that one thing they were fighting for was the right to drink it. Coca-Cola became an international metonym for Americanness. As Sidney Mintz reminds us, before the war Coca-Cola, confined to the southern states, was not a national drink except, at most, as a mixer in alcoholic drinks. During the war, George Catlett Marshall, U.S. Army Chief of Staff and a man of the South, not only persuaded the company to open new bottling plants to furnish the troops, but saw to it that Coca-Cola production had the same status as army food provisions and munitions and was excluded from sugar rationing.

The success of pasta and pizza, the other operation to define and reinforce a national identity, preceded that of Coca-Cola. Italian emigrants found that their fragile identity, barely emergent in its homeland, constricted by the vice-like grip of other identities, was crystallized in the Italian foodstuffs par excellence, the symbolic dishes that eliminated regional differences and the contrast between north and south.

Like Coca-Cola, pasta and pizza became the banner flying over an entire nation and leading it forward.

Foodstuffs as a Threshold or Show Window and the "Cabbage as a Snack" Effect

The fact that food can define a vacillating identity has been observed in other cases as well: Mary Douglas reminds us that whenever a people anticipates invasions and dangers, the dietetic rules that define it as a people are used as a vivid analogy for its endangered cultural categories as a whole.

An immigrant group is an endangered people, and one of the first ways that an immigrant comes face to face with a native population is, quite naturally, through "ethnic" restaurants. Vietnamese, Turks, Tunisians and Algerians, Senegalese, Mexicans, Chinese, and Russians have all begun to make their way in a new society by opening eateries, at first serving customers from within the immigrant community, thus reinforcing ties of identity and kinship, and eventually satisfying the curiosity of outsiders. This "low identity threshold" is a wasteland in which a harmless exchange can take place between the new arrivals and the host country. Here curiosity is satisfied and reciprocal stereotypes exchanged, dramatizing the differences between the groups but ultimately serving the purposes of both groups. This sets up a misunderstanding (as I have stated elsewhere) that nevertheless leaves room for translation. Cookery is the most accessible threshold in this intercultural sampling. There is no need to learn the other's language or culture; all it takes is to believe—or blithely assume—that the dishes tasted are "characteristic."

I have already mentioned the unfortunate "cabbage as a snack" effect. It dictates that ethnic restaurants are always a falsification, a misunderstanding in which both parties agree not to take themselves seriously. The customers want to eat "typical" or "authentic" dishes and the restaurant owners furnish "authentic" and "typical" dishes that match the customers' expectations. This permits visiting another people's cuisine with the illusion of a genuine voyage to sample their tastes. The trip is largely illusory, however, because to enter into the alimentary system of the tastes and preferences of other cultures requires the acquisition of a competence based on the daily frequentation of a cultural, geographical, and alimentary milieu.

There are extremes in every alimentary culture beyond which curiosity about another cuisine turns to disgust. Such personal limits can involve hot peppers or insipidity, gelatinous substances or decomposing mystery items, insupportable odors or sickening sweetness. In spite of this, a curiosity concerning other cuisines also arises from the temptation connected with disgust, and a visit to a culture by means of its cooking is a highly useful and tranquilizing exercise in tolerance. Even in a falsified form for consumption by outsiders, cookery is the most accessible, most easily sampled threshold to another culture.

Coca-Cola and Pasta Again, With a Little Help From My Friends

For Americans soldiers serving overseas in World War II, Coca-Cola fulfilled the very helpful purpose of fostering identification with something simple and immediate. A beverage or a food can serve as a stereotype to cling to, and it helps conceal awkward and poorly defined differences.

Where pasta and pizza are concerned, the American Army is replaced by the mass of Italian immigrants: instead of generals, we have Neapolitan (and, soon, emigrant) entrepreneurs. The same ships that carried future consumers of pasta also carried energetic men with names like La Rosa, Caruso, or Tampieri—pasta-makers who soon realized that durum wheat grown in Canada or the United States could be used to produce *in loco* pasta similar to Italian imports.

One exemplary story is that of Ettore Boiardi, who was working as a cook in Piacenza in 1910 when he met the famous tenor, Enrico Caruso. Caruso invited Boiardi to come to America. In New York he worked as a chef at the Knickerbocker Hotel, then at the Plaza. He cooked for President Wilson at an official dinner, and eventually he opened his own restaurant, "Il Giardino d'Italia," in Cleveland.

The success of Boiardi's restaurant led to a demand for pasta dishes to take home, so he began to can spaghetti with tomato sauce and Parmesan cheese. Production soon rose to an industrial scale, and Boiardi added the famous canned ravioli, changing his name, judged difficult to pronounce, to "Chef Boy-Ar-Dee."

The American Army used his canned pasta as rations, with the result that his face on the label made him one of the most easily recognized men in the United States. Boiardi died a wealthy man at the age of 87 in Parma, Ohio (an ironic geographical coincidence if there ever was one).

From Ethnic Food to Just Food

But I am getting ahead of myself. As Jack Goody reminds us, pasta began to be so widely consumed in the United States that by 1890 an American not of Italian origin named Frank Foulds was manufacturing dry pasta on an industrial scale, guaranteeing its quality by stating on the labeled package, "manufactured with care for Americans."

Here our stories intertwine and multiply. What happened is that pasta, which had begun as an "ethnic" dish consumed by one immigrant group, became widespread and recognized throughout America.

Among other things, it was in America that the legend that spaghetti originated in China and was brought to Italy by Marco Polo got its start. *Il milione* states only that in Fanfur (in Sumatra) Marco Polo ate a dough product made with flour from the bread tree. After processing, "various kinds of eatables are made, such as cakes, and so forth, of the kind that we prepare with wheat-flour."

Marco Polo dictated *Il milione* to Paolo Rustichello in Pisa in 1298, and, as we have already seen, twenty-one years earlier the Genoese notary,

Ugolino Scarpa, had already mentioned macaroni while writing up a will. Thus the legend of the Chinese origin of pasta is highly unlikely to be true.

Whatever the facts may be, the story was repeated in the *Macaroni Journal* in 1928, where a sailor on Marco Polo's voyage named "Spaghetti" gained possession of directions for making pasta in Cathay. In 1938 Lula Beth Maxwell published a more romantic version of the discovery of pasta in the same *Macaroni Journal*:

> There is the story, mythical of course, of the Chinese maid who was busy one day mixing a batch of bread dough in the shade of a large tree. Her secret lover, an Italian sailor who was a member of the famous Marco Polo expedition to the Orient, made so ardent love to her that she completely forgot her task. A gust of wind blew some leaves from the tree into the bowl of dough. On seeing this the pretty Chinese maid, fearful of the scolding that was coming to her for her carelessness and the wasting of the priceless flour, knew not what to do. Her lover came to the rescue. He conceived the idea of straining the leaves out of the mixture by forcing the dough through a rough sieve—the maid's wicker basket. The dough protruded in thin strands, dried quickly in the sun while the lovers continued their lovemaking. Not knowing what to do with the dried strings of dough the maid presented them to her lover, who took them to his ship, boiled them in broth and found them most edible. On his return to Italy Marco Polo had his chef prepare some of this "pasta," the new wheat food, for the nobility of that nation, who tasted, approved, and adopted it as the food of the nation.

Thus was introduced into that country the art of macaroni making long before Columbus discovered America.

In the early twentieth century, Italian emigration was still largely aimed at the United States, reaching a high between 1906 and 1910, when 41% of Italian emigrants chose the United States (though Argentina and Brasil also experienced massive Italian immigration during the same years). According to Robert Foerster, at its height, Italian immigrants counted for 7.4% of the population of New York, 20% of the population of Buenos Aires, and 35% of that of São Paulo. This exodus was not only massive but mobile. Of the 26 million Italians who emigrated from 1876 to 1976, 8.5 million returned to Italy between 1905 and 1976.

The emigrants' mobility made them act as catalysts in economic movements, the redistribution of goods, and changing tastes. It was almost as if they were entrepreneurs—another reason for viewing them as opening the world market for pasta. To be sure, the success of Italians abroad often followed hard times, when Italians were looked down on as "spaghetti-eaters," before being recognized as the people whose "Mediterranean cuisine" had become chic fare and was considered health food. But—and this is the point—food, always an occasion for generalization, gave Italians a place in the American imaginary.

In the film, *Big Night*, Stanley Tucci and Campbell Scott show how this process works. Two brothers from Abruzzo, Primo and Secondo (and I shall return in the last chapter to these men with sharply metaphorical names) run a restaurant in New Jersey in the 1950s. Their customers are incapable of appreciating the philological wealth of Primo's cooking. They cannot understand it—and how could they?—or penetrate the nuances of what Primo considers the only possible cuisine because it is his cuisine, the cookery in which he is profoundly imbedded, with which he is deeply imbued. Secondo is a little more "advanced," and even though he acknowledges that his brother has his reasons, he knows that Primo is not right in their new situation, where food has to be translated for an American public. The English that the brothers speak stresses their difference: Primo's English is rudimentary, a pidgin, the minimum needed for self-defense and understanding the basics; Secondo speaks an English of seduction. He wants to become part of the culture that surrounds him. The brothers define a barrier separating the purity of local tradition from a desire to discover, mix, and reinvent. Across the street from their restaurant a Sicilian named Pascale has understood the whole situation much better. His highly successful restaurant gives Americans the stereotype of Italy that they want: red and white checked tablecloths, candles stuck into Chianti bottles, and spaghetti and meatballs (a dish that does not exist in Italy).

The conflict outlined in the film is unresolvable. "True" local traditional cooking can be appreciated only by "natives." If others are to appreciate it, it must cease somehow to be "authentic" and indigenous. What succeeds is not local and regional cooking, which is complex and nuanced. It is not the drum-shaped *timballo abruzzese*, but a vulgarization of regional cooking, re-mixed and flattened to a homogeneity not found in its original form.

Cuisine à la Bignami or à la Thomas Bowdler and the Invention of Italian Cooking

In the culinary sphere, the simplification now known as "bowdlerization" (from Bowdler's 1818 attempt to rewrite Shakespeare's works, purging them of the passages he held to be vulgar or debatable) may offend the more refined cook and invite scorn, but it enables someone who has already made the transition into another culture to understand that what is going on is the invention of a new tradition.

In reality, what Pellegrino Artusi accomplished for Italy was also a "bowdlerization" (or a version resembling Bignami cram notes for school examps) editing Italian cooking, expurgating it of its context, and reducing it to the level of a more general, broader public. In a certain sense, Artusi's cookbook is a *Reader's Digest* treatment of Italian regional cuisine. The term, "to bowdlerize" has been used today to explain how the menus of Chinese or Italian restaurants function out of their native lands. Artusi's efforts were successful because, if Italy was to be unified, it had to be demonstrated that there was a national cuisine as well as a national literature.

Jack Goody, Mary Douglas, and Sidney Mintz, who have studied the question of "national cuisines," agree on this point: no national cuisines exist as such. A people has need of such a thing only in moments of sweeping political change. Mary Douglas says that a national cuisine helps to trace the limits of a political identity, and in order to create it, that people mixes, drastically compacts, and bowdlerizes regional and local cuisines. Mintz is even more categorical:

> A national cuisine is a contradiction in terms; there can be regional cuisines, but not national ones. I think that for the most part, a national cuisine is simply a holistic artifice based on the foods of the people who live inside some political system, such as France or Spain. "Cuisine," more exactly defined, has to do with the ongoing foodways of a region, within which active discourse about food sustains both common understandings and reliable production of the foods in question. Haute cuisine, so called, is some sort of refinement of the aggregate foods, styles, and dishes of a collection of regions, a skimming off of representative foods to create a cuisine that is national by virtue of being widely representative. Haute cuisine differs from cuisine by representing more than one region, by adding expensive substitutions in the foods themselves, and sometimes by acquiring international status. It is, like it or not, "restaurant food," of the sort that turns up in restaurants abroad, and in capital cities.

Thus Italian cooking was invented, just as though nothing of the sort had ever existed. When Italian cookery returned from the United States, Italy found itself endowed with a national cuisine.

Inextricably Italian-American

The creation of an Italian cuisine arose from a specific encounter between Italian domesticity and the standardization model and the shop-window effect of a great and expanding American market. It could be said that the Italians rode that model so masterfully that they made Italianness appealing and salable worldwide.

In the difficult process of a struggle for survival, Italians abroad made their way, even very well, and in fact much better than many other immigrant groups, because they "speculated" on the stereotype that the New World attributed to them. "Made in Italy" was created in just this way. Pasta and pizza were the matrix after which other operations were modeled. "Food Italian Style" anticipated "Italian Fashion" and "The Italian Way of Film-Making."

In Woody Allen's film, *Sleeper*, an absent-minded Diane Keaton tells Allen, who wakens to find himself in the year 2020, that the world has changed and all sexual problems have been resolved. Everyone is frigid, and all men except those of Italian descent have become impotent. Allen exclaims that he has always known there was something special about pasta.

The Italian Peninsula never had any great admiration for its émigrés, however. Italy soon forgot that half of its population had emigrated, and it treated its co-nationals with derision, laughing at their awkwardness. The Italian-American became a stereotype in the eyes of the true Italian, who, in an ironic reversal, was unaware that it was precisely the Italian-Americans who had created the stereotype by which Italians—even those who remained in Italy—were recognizable as such.

John Fante, the author of *Wait Until Spring, Bandini*, has written extensively about emigration. In several of his novels he depicts the force of a dual cuisine—a maternal force—compacted and oppressed by circumstances, but which provides the substratum of living in an America in which Italy is a Rome yearned for but never experienced.

If we glance at current tourist guides to Italy we can find statements that confirm a vision of Italianness based on home and domesticity. The 1997 *Rough Guide* (published in London) insists that Italy continues to boast a domestic and regional cuisine and that the Peninsula is free of trends and untouched by the near-global mania for health foods ("No whole wheat pizza"). The 1997 Australian guide *Lonely Planet* speaks of the "question of *al dente* pasta," as something known and debated by all Italians with a competence shared throughout the land.

Spaghetti vs. Barbarity

While the Italian-American was caricatured in Italian films of the 1960s, where he coexisted with the Americanized Italian stigmatized by Alberto Sordi, in the United States the "Italian way" began to dictate what was in good taste and what was barbarous.

In one of the most extraordinary documents of American civilization, a Galateo created by Judith Martin speaking as "Miss Manners," the very definition of civilization hangs on the question of spaghetti.

The "spaghetti problem" prompts an impassioned debate under the heading, "Spaghetti" in a chapter on table manners in the lengthy tome, *Miss Manners' Guide to Excruciatingly Correct Behavior*. A reader asks "Miss Manners": "How do you eat spaghetti with a spoon?" She replies:

> Gentle Reader: Bite your tongue. This is not an eating instruction, but an old-fashioned reprimand to anyone who would even entertain such an outrageous idea as eating spaghetti with a spoon. Actually, there simply is no easy, foolproof way to eat spaghetti, and that is just as well when you think of how gloriously fat we would all be if there were. The inevitable slippage of spaghetti from the fork back onto the plate is Nature's way of controlling human piggishness. A fork is the only utensil that may be used to eat spaghetti while anyone is looking. It must make do with whatever cooperation it may muster from the plate and the teeth. The fork is planted on the plate, and the spaghetti is then twirled around the tines of the fork. If you can manage to use the grated cheese to add grit to the mixture for better control, so much the better. The twirled forkful is then presented to the mouth. If this were an ideal world, all the spaghetti strands would begin and end in the same place, so that the mouth could receive the entire forkful at once. However, we have all learned that compromises must often be made, and the fact is that one will often find a few long strands hanging down outside

the mouth. As you may not spit these parts back onto the plate, what are you to do with them? Well, for heaven's sake. Why do you think God taught you to inhale?

That does not end the matter, however. The questioner responds:

> Dear Miss Manners: Eating spaghetti is a two-handed exercise and it does employ the use of a spoon. But consider first your proposed method, the fork perched like a flagpole on the place, twirling the spaghetti around its base as though to drill a hole in the china. Ugh. Proper, perhaps, for a Roto-Rooter man. The correct way to eat spaghetti is with a fork and a soup spoon. The soup spoon is held in the right hand, the fork in the left. One cannot eat spaghetti properly without a soup spoon. Shame on you.

And of course Miss Manners replies:

> Gentle Reader: That many people use spoons to assist forks in eating spaghetti, Miss Manners is well aware. That correct spaghetti eating, with fork only, is not easy, Miss Manners is well aware. (Why Miss Manners is suddenly writing her sentences backward, she also does not know.) The most rewarding things in life require patience and diligence. In the civilized world, which includes the United States and Italy, it is incorrect to eat spaghetti with a spoon. The definition of "civilized" is a society that does not consider it correct to eat spaghetti with a spoon.

The World of Pasta and Pizza

The boom of spaghetti (and pasta in general) in the United States has been so overwhelming that despite a thriving pasta production in America, the importation of Italian pasta continues to elicit worry and protectionist sentiment from Americans.

On the one hand, the Vitelli firm, located in New York City, produces pasta and canned tomato products, grossing some $15 million annually and using tomatoes from Chile and pasta made in Turkey. The United States is the biggest producer of pasta after Italy, with an annual output of two million tons a year. Importation from Italy remains sizable, however, representing a total dollar value (in 1995) of some $119 million.

The American pasta industry complains of the low retail cost of Italian pasta, which it considered unfair competition for a constantly growing American demand for pasta that has increased from 7 kilos per person per year in 1980 to 14 kilos today.

Although pasta functioned in the United States to open the way to a broader acceptance of things Italian, its spectacular success did not stop at that. Also according to the Barilla company's media relations office, forty-four countries produce pasta world-wide today, for a total of 11.5 million tons a year. Italy leads the list of consumers of the Mediterranean variety of dried pasta, with 28 kilos per capita annually, followed by Venezuela (12.6 kilos per capita), Tunisia (11.7 kilos), Switzerland (9.8 kilos), Greece (9.6 kilos), the United States (9 kilos), and

Ireland (1 kilo). Africa eats much more pasta than it used to, and entire African countries have substituted it for rice or millet.

What explains that success? And why did the same thing not happen with couscous, Chinese noodles, *paella valenciana*, or polenta? Why, within a fifty-year period, did a commodity typical of a regional and local cuisine become a foodstuff widely used, and not only by restaurants, to the point of becoming a product that could be bought uncooked and prepared at home? For what reason did that "ethnic" dish stop being ethnic, so that we are not surprised if a German should choose to cook spaghetti at home, while it seems to us strange, acceptable only on an experimental basis, if an Italian makes couscous or an American stirs up a pot of polenta? How did it happen that making hamburgers at home is not as common an occurrence in Italy as cooking pasta in the United States? Pasta has become a universal foodstuff, even though it remains connected with its cultural derivation from Italy. Something different happened to pizza, which has become so universal that it has lost all trace of its origins, as we shall see at the end of this chapter.

One reason for the sweeping success of pasta is undoubtedly the ease with which it can be cooked. Pasta is widely present in lands of rapid urbanization (Somalia, Guatemala, and many African lands, for instance) because it is harder to find low-cost fuel in the city than in the country. Some cereals or other substances that require slow cooking become very costly in energy. Pasta cooks in only a few minutes, resulting in a saving of cooking gas, an expensive item for newcomers to the city.

Another reason for the success of pasta is its long shelf life. Pasta is semi-processed, easy to package and transport, and ready to cook. Thus it fits perfectly among the foods that make up a large part of African and Latin American cooking: just like rice, millet, corn, sagum, or manioc, it is a base to which a sauce or an accompaniment can be added.

In Cuba during the "special period" of the embargo and meager harvests, pasta was one of the few available resources for many Cubans. Even in the Chiapas of Marcos and the Zapatistas, Indian women today cook pasta as if it were a typical part of the daily diet. The local women were surprised when Italian women visiting the Zapatista camps boiled water for pasta, because for them pasta is first sautéd with chopped onion and garlic, like rice for risotto, and only when it has browned is boiling water added.

If pasta's nutritive qualities explain some of its success, there are other, more symbolic reasons. Among them is that it seems "hygienic" (also one of the reasons for Coca-Cola's rise in the Third World) and "civilized"—that is, it does not appear to be a "raw material." There may also be the allure of Western colonization, in which Italy and America are viewed as one. All of these enter into a globalization in which agricultural countries, producers of raw materials, are dependent upon Western countries that produce raw materials at a lower cost, thanks to more efficient production methods and the perverse mechanisms of an unequal exchange.

The fact remains, however, that world-wide, pasta consumption is rising at a dizzying pace. It is not a high-fashion foodstuff, but a popular one, in the sense of widely present rather than specific to humble folk, although it is true that its broad distribution is closely linked to its image as a food for everyone.

What is even more impressive is that in Africa, in Latin America, and in Asia, pasta has acquired the status of a daily foodstuff, rather than just being a way to fill up occasionally. This takes us back to the question of satiety, in relation to which Sereni observes that pasta not only fed the Neapolitan lower classes but satisfied them as well. Even today, in many places throughout the world, the "full stomach" effect gives pasta an edge as the most immediate response to pangs of hunger and fatigue.

Has Italian Cooking Become *Haute Cuisine*?

In Western lands pasta has a different history. Originally part of the domestic *koinè* represented by Italians abroad, pasta went through a long incubation period during which it was considered "good cooking," for "simple and frugal tastes," or "Mamma's cooking," eventually rising, in the United States in particular, to the level of *haute cuisine*, in part because it was associated with health foods and the rediscovery of regional cooking. Jack Goody's classic work, *Cooking, Cuisine and Class*, teaches us that a *haute cuisine* arises out of political and social change. Regional cuisines contribute to the rise of a national cuisine thanks to ingredients, cooking methods, and dishes drawn from regional cuisines that become the repertory of "chefs" who cook for people whose competence, taste, and objectivity transcend any single locality. This generally happens in a capital city (or a court), where the clients are powerful and privileged.

This means that in the United States today, Italians of the second and third generation cook pasta for their American friends as a sign of their own rise in status. The more their status improves, the more Italianness can be taken as a sign of class rather than origin. This is the conclusion of a group of scholars of Italian-American culture, as presented in a dissertation by Janet Schwarz Theophano under the title, "It's Really Tomato Sauce But We Call it Gravy." Italians who have made great efforts to become integrated and to get ahead in American society find, once they have "arrived," that they can use cooking to show off their origins, to the fascination of the local elite who are their invited guests.

Haute cuisine is a term applied to two major and historical culinary traditions, those of China and of France, lands in which court cuisine was soon transformed into "chef's" cuisine. In China a thousand years ago, the cuisine of other parts of the Celestial Empire could be enjoyed in the bigger cities.

Italy presents a different picture. It is precisely the more "modest," homey nature of the Italian cooking invented in America that transformed it from an ethnic cuisine into a *haute cuisine*, exaggerating the very characteristics of "simple," and "sober" cooking (or "Mamma's cooking"), and taking sublime advantage of the ideological trend toward "simple living."[5] Similar things happened in fashion from the 1950s to today, when designers imitating the "Prince of Wales" style switched to street style—that is, young people's clothing and street people's clothing—a change signaled by the welcome given to the figure of Marlon Brando and his leather jacket in the film *The Wild One*.

If exclusive restaurants like Chez Panisse in Berkeley—restaurants that founded a school of cuisine and produced a manual—move from French dishes or *nouvelle cuisine* to Italian cooking, managing to sell "Italian-style" deep-dish pizza as a chic food, it means that "Italian cooking" has become accepted as a definition of distinction. A man will take his date to eat in an Italian restaurant, not a French one. This new state of affairs mimics the transformation of pasta's image in recent decades: once a popular food and a "national" dish, it now enjoys internationally recognized status, just like Dolce and Gabbana clothes or a Prada purse. This last shift corresponds to the inclusion of cookery

---

[5]It is interesting to note that in France the 1996 Millau guide to ethnic cuisine places Italian cooking among them. France seems to establish a desperate defense against the globalization of Italian cooking by "putting it in its place" in an ethnic niche. The operation is somewhat paradoxical, as it reflects the failure of French *haute cuisine* to make the leap forward to globalization that would assure its future. This is all rather surprising, if we think that in France itself the trend today is to brasseries and restaurants serving *moules et frites*. Sauerkraut (*choucroute*) and mussels with fries hardly seem worthy of a great tradition. Americans lent a hand by dubbing deep-fried potatoes "French fries," but the French seem not to have profited from the fact. The French still have *crêpes*, however, which have become the real French fast food, but I don't think that Gault and Millau would be delighted. I am indebted to Ciro Polge, an excellent Italian cook in France, for these thoughts.

within the field of taste (as a "distinction," as Pierre Bourdieu would say) that signifies that pasta "represents" its origin as if it were a fashionable brand name.

This shift is something extremely recent, but it is occurring with other "origins" as well—that is, with cooking of Mexican origin (or, better, "Tex-Mex") or Japanese origin (the sushi bar). Here terms like "ethnic" or "national" do not represent a real (or even presumed) authenticity of origin (as in truly ethnic restaurants—Lebanese, Cuban, Thai—that feel they have to proclaim themselves "authentic"). An Italian restaurant, a Tex-Mex one, or a sushi bar can be run by someone who is not Italian, neither Texan nor Mexican, and not Japanese, without causing any problem for the customer.

What diners are seeking is the universalization of a brand name. This is not just a marketing trick to falsify the various cuisines (as though there were an authentic Italian cuisine, and as if all Italian restaurants abroad were not false in any event). Rather, what happens is a creolization of a cuisine that already makes a display of its translation into a universal, multiethnic language, hence is in fieri.

Pasta, pizza, and Italian cooking have stood at the forefront of this process. Italian restaurants abroad have moved in the direction of creating a menu that is a pidgin, a *lingua franca* of restaurant-speak.

The Creolization of Cuisine

Anyone who travels the world today will begin to find restaurants that declare no ethnic bent, but already reflect the mixture of two alimentary cultures in a new international cuisine that offers a certain level of quality derived more from techniques than from recipes.

In San Francisco, for example, right next to The Stinking Rose, an elegant restaurant that proclaims itself extremely Italian because everything it offers is loaded with garlic (even the ice cream), there is another super-chic restaurant called The House, where Chinese and Japanese chefs prepare dishes "all'italiana," in the sense that the cooking times and the ingredients are those of a cuisine *all'italiana* but the recipes are usually Asiatic.

This is a highly interesting development. The mixture is possible because domestic Japanese cooking much resembles the cooking of an Italian Mamma and features simple dishes that rely on carefully cooked and healthy foods. The House is betting on this similarity since, not coincidentally, it is located in North Beach, a section of San Francisco that is historically Italian.

Emigration is a rich source of misunderstanding: it involves an interesting process of invention, but also a reversal of identity. Once the process has begun, it is hardly surprising to see Tunisians dressed as Sicilians running a pizzeria in Aci Trezza, or ex-Yugoslavs opening an Italian restaurant in San Francisco and calling it "Michelangelo." Nor should we be surprised by a story that Paolo Monelli tells in his *Ghiottone errante* (1935). Finding himself in

Palermo, Monelli meets a cook just returned to Sicily, who tells him, "Jéa, sono stato tre anni a Nuova Jorca, a Bronx Park—sciòa." The Sicilian came home because he was tired of encountering Sicilians and Amalfitans everywhere, and had opened a tavern in Palermo where at least once in a while he saw a foreigner.

Chauvinism *al dente*

This said, "true" Italians still had to surmount the chauvinistic pleasure of thinking that no one else eats as well as they and get over the habit of avoiding all restaurants abroad that are not Italian or a pizzeria. Surpassed perhaps only by the Japanese, Italians are the first clients of "their own" restaurants abroad, although they soon discover that you don't eat in them as you do in Italy.

Ugo Tognazzi has described this cultural chauvisism better than anyone in his account of a gigantic *spaghetti alla carbonara* that he himself prepared for three hundred fifty guests invited to the Hilton Hotel in New York for the opening of the 1965 film *Marcia Nuziale* (The Wedding March). His description of having to judge how much time it would take to transport his *carbonara* by elevator from the basement kitchens to the top floor ballroom without having the egg mixture set too much is a glorious gag, and his explanation of why he chose to do a *carbonara* in the first place is a masterpiece of alimentary confusion.

I went back to the guest list to study it a bit. Americans, almost all of them. Crazily American. I had to decide what type of spaghetti to prepare. I began by rapidly reviewing the various types of *pastasciutta* in my mind to see which might best please the Yankee palate. I immediately eliminated *spaghetti al pomodoro e basilico* because they might have thought it was pizza. I didn't have time to prepare a *ragù*, which would scarcely have been a novelty for them anyway. I rejected *all'amatriciana* by reason of legitimate doubts concerning American canned tomatoes. By a process of elimination I arrived at *alla carbonara*. A *carbonara* might not disappoint them, because it is our pasta style closest to United States tastes. Where could anyone find two foods more genuinely American than fried bacon and beaten eggs? Naturally, I thought I wouldn't stop there. I would add some cream, which Americans put into everything, and, at the last minute, a bit of alcohol, which, after all, finally has an heading of its own today in new American criteria for blood analysis. And what is pasta if not processed wheat? Isn't that what American sandwiches are? We Italians see pasta as a product somewhere between a threat and a magic formula, a miraculous foodstuff that God sent down to Earth to console us for our many Italic shortcomings. But when all is said and done, if we want to reason about it, isn't it just bread made in another way?

And What About Pizza?

Sidney Mintz tells us,

> The list of ten favorite lunch and dinner "entrées"
> for 1994, collected by the NPD market research
> group, starts off with pizza and ham sandwiches and
> hot dogs, and ends with cheese sandwiches,
> hamburger sandwiches, and spaghetti.

Lee Iacocca states in his autobiography that when he was a boy in the Bronx, he told his friends that in Italy people ate something called "pizza" that was something like a pie, but with tomatoes on top. The other boys laughed at him because they couldn't believe that there could be a pie with tomatoes on top. Does this mean that "pizza pie" has not always existed in America? In spite of what Americans may think now, pizza arrived, more or less like pasta, from Italy and at a specific time. Although the story of its place of origin is clear in the case of pasta, we know less about that of pizza.

We need to think of pasta and pizza as two different things, even if they have had a similar success and world-wide diffusion. Pizza, as we have seen, became the more public food; it was street food, something to be eaten outside of the home. It became the alternative to a hamburger. In short, it became the public dimension of Italianness, and it kept its popular appeal as a food that is cheap and relatively easy to make.

At the start, pizzerias in America and elsewhere created an urban landscape in which Italy, rather than responding to *haute cuisine* by creating a high cuisine of its own, invented widespread distribution. It had an ample tradition to draw upon. Pizza—whether by the name of *piada*, *schiacciata*, or *pizza*—was a simple dish. It was a food that could be rolled out easily, cooked quickly, and eaten "on the go." Pasta required an extra process, drying, which in turn depended on a production phase, pre-industrial or industrial.

Pizza and pasta possess two opposed characteristics where the Italian identity is concerned. Pizza is frugality made rich and inventive, but it is so simple that its Italian origin overlooked. America soon appropriated it. Pasta comes in many varieties, hence it is the contrary of simplicity. Its existence requires the existence of the entire catalog of pasta types. To eat a plate of pasta signifies entry into a classifying system (a question to which I shall return in the next chapter) and inclusion within the Italian culinary system; this does not happen to someone who just eats a pizza. Pizza is the only daughter of a desire for variety. Pasta is a trap of multiplicity; it ambushes the consumer by the fact that one variety cannot be enjoyed fully without knowing the others. The paradox of pasta is that pasta is much more similar to a cultural system than pizza is.

Pizza is like a manufactured object from an archaeological age of which we have lost all other trace. It is that archaeological quality that enables pizza to shake off its geographical origin and gives it a place within the landscape of the big city, in locales that offer easily prepared poor foods and that are located next to places offering shish kabob, shawarma, Tunisian sand-wiches, gyros, and pita bread with falafel. There should be nothing surprising about discovering that the Turks have their own pizza, and that some inexpensive Turkish or Iranian eateries are called "Pizza Istanbul" or "Pizza Parsi." Or that all lands (but Mediterranean lands in particular) have created an extraordinarily convenient food made of a flat piece of baked wheat-and-water dough topped with tomato, ground meat, or just a tasty herb or spice.

As a street food: pizza escapes the tyranny of the tablecloth and the table and liberates the traveler from the dread of the bill. In this sense, pizza is more universal, more cosmopolitan, and more closely tied to relativism than is pasta. Moreover, behind the fact that America claims paternity for it (pizza has become to all effects one of the symbols of Americanness, along with hamburgers and fast food in general) there lies the profound mystery of a foodstuff that may belong to no one. Like the myth of Oedipus or the story of Faust, it is something of an archetype. Today, near a fairgrounds, in the seedier districts of the city, or near the entertainment quarters; along the crowded streets of Broadway or in the Arab quarters of Paris, pizza is a stateless world citizen, claimed by one nationality or another just as Lebanese, Turks, Greeks, Jews, and Arabs dispute ownership of shawarma or falafel.

Where pizza becomes aristocratic is in lands without wheat, such as Japan. There it reacquires an ethnic dimension strong enough to remove it from the "take-out" connotations of Pizza Hut and to guarantee its "Italian authenticity" by the mere mention of the name "Pizza La," the largest Japanese chain of take-out pizza. Recently, an entire issue of the Japanese fashion magazine *Brutus* was dedicated to a "pizza police" operation. A group of "authentic Neapolitan pizzaioli" dressed as real Italians—that is, as Italian-Americans of the gangster variety—traveled through the streets of Tokyo in a Fiat Cinquecento, inspecting all the pizzerias to make sure that the quality of their pizza was up to par.

Italians abroad can exercise their chauvinism by avoiding local cookery and taking refuge in a pizzeria, be it independent or part of a chain. They are persuaded that in any event a pizza is not going to be inedible and that, since it is a simple dish, you can get away with spending the minimum, with little risk of disappointment. The Pizza Pino outlets in France are crowded, and throughout Europe there are Pizza Huts happy to serve carry-out customers. Pizza seems destined to become reliant on packaging. You receive a pizza in a box, and you eat it out of the box. This presents some non-Italians with a serious problem of etiquette, as Miss Manners reminds us. A reader writes:

Dear Miss Manners: What is the proper way to serve carry-out Chinese food or pizza? I don't want you to think that I don't know how to serve a proper meal that I cook myself, but what about impromptu gatherings, when you just send out for something? Should I try to pass it off as mine—which is difficult if everybody hears the doorbell ring when it's delivered—or should I just put it out the way it arrives?

Miss Manners replies:

> Gentle Reader: Many Americans are under the mistaken impression that small paper cartons with metal handles are correct serving dishes in China (or Taiwan), and that large flat cardboard boxes are in Italy. Transfer the carry-out food into your own serving dishes. This does not imply that you cooked it yourself. The cow gets credit for having produced the milk, even if it is put into a glass before serving."

Once again, Italy functions as a protection against barbarity.

III
Childhood: A Digression

The kitchen. La cucina, the true mother country, this warm cave of the good witch deep in the desolate land of loneliness, with pots of sweet potions bubbling over the fire, a cavern of magic herbs, rosemary and thyme and sage and oregano, balm of lotus that brought sanity to lunatics, peace to the troubled, joy to the joyless, this small twenty-by-twenty world, the altar a kitchen range, the magic circle a checkered tablecloth where the children fed, the old children, lured back to their beginnings, the taste of mother's milk still haunting their memories, fragrance in the nostrils, eyes brightening, the wicked world receding as the old mother witch sheltered her brood from the wolves outside.

—John Fante, *The Brotherhood of the Grape*

I have never seen much of Gardel. When he stopped in front of me at the Ambassador, he asked me about Dandy. We organized a rehearsal at home. He came, like a young gentleman, at the agreed upon hour. I had invited him to eat a fine minestrone, and he had responded, "Young Man, all the Argentines invite me to eat minestrone. What is your mother, Italian, Gallega?" I had answered that she was Italian. "In that case, I want to eat pasta," he answered. We agreed that he would come and eat a plate of ravioli. He came to us the next day, and while my mother was in the kitchen tending to the ravioli, I sang *Dandy* to him, and he said to her: "Mind you, this piece is by your son, and I will score a fine goal with it."

—Osvaldo Soriano,
"Lucio Demare: El tango del Abasto a París"

How can I define the personal role of pasta and pizza—
not its role in my own life, but its biographical role, its
part in the life of all Italians when they talk about pasta
and pizza? If I were a Creole or Mexican writer I would
devote pages to the smells and tastes of childhood, to
the whole atmosphere that enveloped the way the
women of the house cooked, and so on. I would try to
tell about pasta and pizza as Patrick Chamoiseau, the
Creole writer who lives in Martinique, speaks about the
chocolate of his childhood:

> Chocolat première communion
> l'écrire c'est saliver
> y penser c'est souffrir
> communier c'est chocolat

(First Communion Chocolat
to write it is to salivate
to think of it is to suffer
to commune is chocolate; Volk translation)

But we are dealing with a different constellation here. The pasta of my own childhood was not a specialty of one Italian region; it was a way of taking nourishment from an entire culture. It is as if someone asked a Japanese to tell about his experience with rice (*Rice as Self* is the title of Ohnuki-Tierney's excellent study of rice as an integral part of the Japanese identity). This means that it is unlikely that pasta (or rice) leaves a memory separate from other memories, some sort of madeleine whose distinctive but light taste can be reconstructed.

Still, it is possible to say that there is a history of one's own relationship with pasta. When did I eat it for the first time? Who knows? This is like asking a child when he spoke his first words: "Mamma," "ball," "dog." Pasta is part of a patrimony formed in the earliest years of life. Is there a particular pasta dish that I remember? One that left an indelible mark on my life? Not even. There is instead a sizzling, a hiss, and an atmosphere of odors and fragrances that has something to do with the preparation of sauces and with the cooking of the pasta itself. There are staircases, windows, balconies from which such odors escape. There are marvelous moments of light that accompany the statement, "I've put the pasta on." There are memories of the first times that our mothers asked us to test whether the pasta was cooked, memories that include a burned tongue, the deft use of a wooden spoon, a stream of tap water to cool down the sample. One of my strongest memories is adding sugar to the sauce. Another is *frittata di pasta* (a sort of pasta omelet), one of the best and most genial dishes for a simple evening meal. The *frittata di pasta* presupposes having a grandmother, and it presupposes the extraordinary experience of being a child and having a favorite food, which is often not a "main" dish but rather an enchanting way of frying up left-over pasta or mixing the *frittata* with fried potatoes, or making a sauce in the pan. Children and childhood in general experience cooking as a "concession," an entry into a temple that is not theirs, and a chance to produce the confusion and mess typical of children. Precisely: the *frittata di pasta* is a *pasticcio* in both senses of the word: it is a pasta dish and it is a mess, something that grand cuisine would find inadmissible. It signifies playing with food, playing with elements, like making mud pies or leaf sauces.

Other memories? The memory of the first *pasta con le sarde* prepared in the company of school friends. This involved difficult and fascinating operations: first the sardines and the wild fennel had to be cooked separately, then the pasta was cooked in the water used for the fennel, and finally browned bread crumbs were added. This was a first experience of something that demands a degree of competence regarding timing, added ingredients, and culinary secrets that come with years of cooking experience. How different this was from the typical *pasta alla carbonara* that accompanied our first dinners with friends in our own homes, before we learned to use garlic, oil, and hot peppers. Nor have I even a vague memory of my own family's pasta or ways of eating pasta as being Sicilian, although it is true that as a child, when I traveled around Italy with my parents, there was often no pasta and the first course was something else: soup, polenta, timbales. Still, pasta was already taken for granted as a code so firm that theorization was not permitted. Memory turns instead to our parents informing us (to our horror) that there are cultures in which pasta is a side dish, that it might be topped with marmalade, or that some restaurants of Northern Europe, France in particular, serve pasta overcooked and glutenous. In memory pasta goes along with childhood stories: *pasta a rotelle*, *penne di zito*, tiny star-shaped pasta. Pasta was still play when the kitchen was given over to childish desecration.

Memories of pizza? Yes, but they are all connected with an early autonomy, with going out with friends with a few coins in our pockets. Pizza Saturdays, when, for the first time, we break the habit of family dinner in favor of the extraordinary ritual of having supper with friends. Pizza reminds me much more of play food, of food that isn't "serious," like Nutella or, today, hamburgers. It is a food that denies the mother, that denies that eating requires a home and a family ambiance. And, like taking a shower instead of a bath, it makes us feel more agile, less baroque, less attached to domestic activities.

IV
Eating and Thinking Like an Italian

Everything appeals to me. My soul grasps everything. We are fortunate... hence we grasp pleasures: they insert themselves in our very being, and sufferings are but accidents. Things seem disposed everywhere to our satisfaction.... We need to persuade man of his felicity, which he is unaware of even when he enjoys it.

—Montesquieu, *Essai sur le goût*

Along with language, the art of cooking defines humanity in its appropriation of itself and the world; moreover, it is one of the languages of human culture by which cultures are constituted, both in their differences and mutual oppositions; finally, the art of cooking is structured like language and obeys the same structural and functional constraints..

—Louis Marin, *Food for Thought*

Taste is precisely the sense that knows and practices multiple and successive approaches: entrances, returns, overlappings, all in a counterpoint of sensation.

—Roland Barthes,
introduction to Brillat Savarin, *Physiologie du goût*

Thanks to the fact that pasta is a staple, it can be compared with the basic foods of other cuisines, rice in Japanese culture, for example, or meat in French culture.

What is strange about pasta as a food is that anyone who eats pasta actually eats pastas, in the plural. That is, pasta has a multiple identity. The French show that they understand this by pluralizing pasta as *les pâtes*. Behind that plural there lies a change in register. Dried pasta is based on one substance, durum wheat flour, but what the Italians eat is an entire gamut of forms of that one substance. That is fairly singular. There are other cultures that vary a basic substance. Rice, for example, appears in Chinese cuisine cooked in different ways and mixed with peas or bits of egg or meat, but in form it changes little.

Admittedly, meat changes its seasoning and cooking method and is presented in pieces or whole. Pasta, however, is an identical substance that takes on a great variety of forms. Italians eat these forms and can distinguish between them with extraordinary skill. Pasta represents the predominance of form over taste.

This is true, however, in the sense that it is the change in form that determines a change in taste. The same sauce, topping, or seasoning, applied to different shapes of pasta, creates a difference in taste. It is as if the Italian palate were specially dedicated to the tactile aspect of cooking: using the mouth and the tongue to sense the consistency, the surface, the texture, the coarseness or softness, the smooth surface or the ridges of the pasta; whether it is hollow or compact, straight or curved, twisted or cork-screwed, round or spindle-shaped, cut perpendicularly or on an angle. The palate, the tongue, and the teeth sense the form of the pasta, and with every bite they reconstitute it, translating vision into touch. This festival of touch becomes taste because it is true that each shape has a different sapidity and that different shapes respond differently to saliva. There is an appetite for form that is extraordinary. It is hard to explain this to someone who has no experience of the entire system. Would you like *maccheroncini* or *farfalle*? Do you feel like having *maltagliati* or *spaghetti*, *vermicelli* or *penne*?

Is eating for form exclusive to Italians? No: there are many other cultures in which food is also form and color; something to be seen. Like the tomato on our pasta, there are Mexican tortillas sprinkled with a red sauce that turns out to be hot peppers.

The unchanging base of the pasta or the corn tortilla is blended by the eye in a visual contrast that anticipates the contrast of taste of freshness or spiciness. Moreover, certain Mexican ice creams seem made solely for the joy of looking at them. Aside from being a system of savors, food is a gastronomic landscape (about which, more later), and every culture seems to have its own.

Where the Italian system is unique, however, is in the broad gamut of forms of one and the same substance. In this the catalog of different forms of pasta could be compared to the many varieties of Japanese sushi, with the notable difference that sushi is a food in which form is just as important as substance and individual pieces are "filled" with different substances (fish or shellfish). What happens with pasta is a good deal stranger. Among other things, even uncooked pasta sets our saliva flowing. We want to eat uncooked pasta because viewing it evokes contact even more than taste.

For this reason, pasta is a self-referential system. You cannot really enjoy one kind of pasta if you do not also know the others. *Les pâtes* indicates that pasta is already a plurality and never should be imagined as one plateful. Each serving is a recall, one element in a system of intertwined references, and a reminder of the other types. Eating pasta signifies entering into a classification system. This is the trap of multiplicity that requires the existence of a catalog of reproducible pastas. A housewife or a restaurant that offered only one form of pasta would soon become a fast-food place (and in fact there are *spaghetterie* of just that sort). As we have already seen, more than pizza, pasta fully represents a cultural system. As Piero Camporesi reminds us,

> We must not forget, in fact, that cooking is the art of combination and interpolation rather than of invention; its processes involve variation more than pure creation; and the history of cooking is basically the story of the morphology of dishes, in which one must distinguish between variable and constant elements.

Systems and Catalogs

The *Pastario, ovvero Atlante delle paste alimentari italiane*, edited by Eugenio Medagliani and Fernanda Gosetti, catalogues a hundred types of pasta, but in the early twentieth century there seem to have been six hundred of them. Gustavo Tragli's *Il lunario della pastaciutta* (1956) catalogues and provides photographs of 298 varieties.

These lists can set us to dreaming. One begins with *acini di pepe, aeroplani, abissine, africanine, agnolini, agnolotti, anchellini, anelletti, anelli, anelli rigati, anellini* (the difference between *anellini* and *anelletti* is defined thus: the first are "a type of family-style pasta of middling size, with a large hole in them that helps them to absorb the sauce"; the second are "very small pastine of Neapolitan origin, smaller than *anelli rigati*, and always cooked in broth). The list continues: *anelloni, animine, anolini, armellette, armelline, arselle* and *arselloni, astri, avemarie, avena,*

avena grande, barbina, bardele, bassetti, bavette, bavettine, bengasini, bigoli, bigui, boccolotti, boccolotti rigati, bombardoni, brichetti, brofadei, bucatini, and on and on. The list concludes with *stelle, stelline, svoltini, strichetti, tagliatelle, tagliatella nervata, tempestine, tempesta, torciglioni, torta di vermicelli, tortellini, tortiglioni grandi, trifogli, tripolini* (which became popular in 1911 because of the Tripolitan War), *tripolini a nochette, trivellini, trivelli, trombette, tubetti, tubettini, tufoli, turbante, turbantino, vermicelli, vuocche 'e vecchia, zero, ziti* (or *zite*), *zitoni, zituane, zuarini.*

Although some varieties of pasta were affected by the campaign for a "national" cuisine, in general this list reflects their regional or local (and, on occasion, event-based) origin. The list is alphabetical, but lists organized by other, less "narrative" criteria were more taxonomic:

1) Long pasta
   a) round and filled: *capelli d'angelo, capellini* (called *fidelini* in Liguria), *vermicellini, spaghetti, spaghettoni, spaghettoni a matasse liguri* (now disappeared), *fidei da panieri...*
   b) tubular: *bucatini, perciatelli, maccheroncelli, mezze zite, zite, zitoni, candele...*
   c) rectangular or lenticular: *bavette, linguine, lingue di passero, tagliarelli, tagliarellini, fettuccine lunghe...*
   d) with jagged or waved edges: *ricciutelle, reginette, lasagne ricche...*
2) Short Pasta
   a) cylinders cut on the bias: *maltagliati, penne, mostaccioli, maccheroni, pennette, pennini*

(all of which can be smooth or ridged);
b) regular cylinders (smooth or ridged): *ditali, ditaloni, maniche, mezze maniche, bombolotti, rigatoni, tortiglioni, cannelloni...*
c) shell-shaped: *lumache, lumaconi, conchiglie, conchiglioni, gnocchi, abissini* . . .
d) elbows: *chifferi, chifferotti, chifferoni, gramigna...*

It is clear from this classification that this is a system in continuous evolution. Certain "taxons" disappear as elements in the system, much like individual animal or vegetal species, while others appear. One example of the latter is a curved short pasta shape known before the great emigration as *gomiti*, but that is listed in Traglia's 1956 catalog as "elbows."

Anthropologists have taught us to understand the "world view" of a given culture on the basis of classifications and the lists that peoples "without writing" draw up of the vegetable and animal worlds around them (and of everything else: shoes, gods, angels, dreams). Epistemology and ethnology have explained to us that the classifying mentality is fundamental to the formation of a society, because imposing order on the world around us is a sign of "understanding it" according to a way of thinking anchored in context and time. Classification corresponds to self-definition—that is, to defining personal identity in respect to the outside world. There is, for instance, a Japanese way of presenting and classifying food that is particular to Japanese culture (to speak, as always, in ample and illicit generalizations). One after the other, sushi or soups, *lamen* or the Japanese version of a *frittata* are reproduced in models that are placed in the front window of the restaurant or the store to help the customer make a choice. Something similar occurs in photographs of sushi used on a menu. An article on pizza that appeared in the Japanese magazine *Brutus* treats the various forms of pizza in a like manner, organizing them and photographing them side by side to display the entire repertory. The same sort of thing happens in the world of pizza regarding oil, oregano, parsley, tomato, mozzarella, mushrooms, prosciutto, and artichokes. These attempts to reconstruct a complete catalog reflect a mindset that positions things by relation and analogy, hierarchy and correspondence.

Pasta as Thought

Can Italian society be understood on the basis of the classificatory system of its varieties of pasta?

That system comprises, as we have seen, a tremendous number of forms. As a system, it continues to vary, but there are strict rules that govern shifts from one form to another. Specific shapes bear names reflecting localities and events. Things become more complicated because other variables enter into the picture, such as the extracts, sauces, pesto, and the various condiments that accompany pasta. Not all items on the list of pasta varieties can be combined with all of the accompaniments.

Short pasta "marries" well with certain things (peas, fava beans) or certain culinary preparations (being baked, sautéed in a pan, served in soup).

Long forms of pasta have a different "conjugal" destiny: lasagna goes well with a ragù sauce; spaghetti with breadcrumbs and anchovies. The question of what accompaniment is appropriate complicates the question of possible combinations almost infinitely. This is why pasta is a world of infinite variety, and at time of barely perceptible changes in combinations relating to both flavor and form. What goes well with what? What conflicts with what? All in the double sense of combined flavors and combined colors and shapes. The seasonings, toppings, and accompaniments raise enormous questions: should they be cooked or uncooked? Of meat or of fish? Moreover, there is the choice between hot and cold—the steaming bowl of pasta in the winter or the fresh summertime cold pasta—and the question of how odors blend and are heightened or lessened according to the shape of the pasta. Which types of pasta require Parmesan cheese or some other sort of grated cheese, and which do not? There is a long debate about whether or not it is blasphemous to sprinkle cheese on pasta and lentils or pasta and beans. An entire network of intersecting parameters exists, to which we should add occasion and presentation: certain moments of the year call for special dishes and a carefully choreographed presentation.

The way in which pasta or pizza should be eaten would require a chapter of its own. For example, should a pizza be eaten from the edge in, or cut into triangular sections, like a cake?

More on Pasta As Thought

By investigating the complex structure of the connection between pasta and thought, we may perhaps discover the secret of a conservatism in which place still plays a major role. The pasta system can tell us about the way innovation is immediately organized to fit within a complex variety that already exists and how, for that very reason, it is "domesticated" by being stripped of any extraneous or foreign characteristics. Is not this talent for bringing things down to fit its own criteria, this domestication, this taking any attempt to establish a colonization from the outside and reducing it to an advisory myth another possible definition of Italianness? Isn't it the very complexity of the system of shapes and tastes that makes that system impermeable to invasion and intrusion?

All of this means that pasta—but also pizza—is an integral part of an alimentary complex that (as we have seen) is strongly rooted in individual regional cuisines. It also means that both pasta and pizza are parts of systems, local or broader, that resist innovation and variation. A cuisine (or the cuisines) that have given rise to pasta and pizza are extremely rigid entities, but ones that are also capable of infinite variation.

Pizza is not far behind pasta in its possibilities for regulated variation. To be sure, the pizza system seems less complex than in the case of pasta and less open to aggression from the outside (although you can get Buffalo wing pizza in Chicago and such aberrations as orange pizza or chocolate pizza). Within the Italian geographical system, however, each region has its traditional variety—*sfincioni*, *schiacciate*, *foccace*, and others. There is a "competence" attached to pizza, based on local know-how and a familiarity with a certain landscape and a certain milieu.

One thing that scholars of alimentation (and foreign visitors) find striking in the various Italian cuisines is that they presuppose a population competent in its own local cuisine. Competence in the kitchen is similar to the linguistic competence of the native speakers. They may not realize it, but no one is better at navigating within a linguistic system, or at introducing innovations into it (not an easy task, however) that are coherent with the whole. This is how Sidney Mintz defines competence in native cuisine:

> Take something simple like bread. In France as in Italy bread is a nearly invariant accompaniment of any meal, and people have strong feelings about how it should taste. They eat it every day, most of them at every meal. This does not mean that there is only one kind of break or that all bread tastes the same, or that people think it should. Rather, how bread tastes, how the dough is prepared and baked, are subjects of sufficient familiarity and importance to be the basis of discourse. Such subjects unite people culturally; and they tend to do so without reference to such things as belonging to one class or another, or having this much or that much formal education. In some ways, that is what's most interesting about cuisine—when people have one, they know what it is without regard to what other people may tell them, *because* they have been eating it (and many of them, preparing it) for all of their lives, and so they can talk about it.

Many Italians are aware of having that competence—because they are Italians—even if it comes out only when they encounter an anomaly. For example, a German friend of mine (whom I hope does not read these lines) offered to host a dinner in the home of mutual friends in Italy and to prepare a pasta dish that he claimed he had learned to make during a trip to the United States. It was spaghetti topped with beans (stewed) and hot peppers (raw). I wondered for a number of days after why my reaction to that recipe had been so negative, and I realized that it was because my German friend somehow supposed that pasta was an open system that welcomes innovation, to the point that one can add another variation to the infinite numbers that already exist.

That is not the case, however. First, spaghetti almost never is served with beans; second, the mixture of raw and cooked is possible for certain ingredients, but not for others (tomato can be served uncooked with certain kinds of pasta, but not other garden vegetables such as eggplant or peppers). Third, the liquid resulting from the mixture of beans and hot peppers recalls nothing recognizable. In short, you can make pasta with Nutella, avocado, or frogs, but until those ingredients have a solid frame of reference to depend on, the result will be something that is simply out of place and beside the point. A cuisine presupposes a permitted territory of variations that only those who speak the language of that cuisine can really know and an "off-limits" that only they can recognize.

In short, "pasta as thought" is an excellent showcase of a people's mentality. Within its composition, complexity, and limits there lies the story, if we are able to read it, of that people's idiosyncracies and imperceptible constancy. There is a picture of a system of sensibilities, understood both as an ability to classify sensations and as an aesthetics of sensations; of what we want food to say to us, make of us, relate to us, leave to us. That picture includes how to read nuances and piquancies, or—and this is something that Italian cooking may share with few others (Lebanese or Persian cooking, that of the Pará of Brasil, for example)—the way that sensations can vary during the consumption of a single dish, thanks to the underlying flavor of spices and the unexpected emergence of the perfume of aromatic herbs. This is the dialectics of parsley, raisins, saffron, basil, wild mint, anise, pepper, and cheeses, whose savors combine with aromas that develop at a certain temperature and are subtler at others. This continuum says much about a sense of taste that dislikes fixity, preferring a tale to be told, and that does not seek confirmation, but rather takes an indirect approach through allusion and a slow flow (or a cascade) between the nose, the tongue, and the palate.

Food and Fashion

The formalism of a cuisine of that sort is so complex that for an outsider it can seem arbitrary. That arbitrary quality resides in a totally domestic reference in which the "we" is identified with the "I" and gives that "I" the illusion of absolute anarchy.

There is a Sicilian proverb that tells us to eat to please ourselves but dress to please others: "Mancia a gusto tuo e vestiti a gusto d'avutri," thus emphasizing the undefinable nature, if not of the individual, at least of the pleasure taken in foods. It is a relic of a world in which how people dressed seemed more rigid than gastronomy.

It is true, however, that even today in Italy, most foods have escaped the change that has struck clothing. Italians follow fashion in their clothes, but not in their eating habits, while elsewhere many follow food fashions ranging from *nouvelle cuisine* to biological, ethnic, and health foods. In this sense, pasta is symbolic of a world—the Italian one—in which the "we" is well defended from external influence and requires lifetime ties with a specific locality. All of that is conservatism and local boosterism, but it is also what foreigners, falling into the trap, call "authenticity" when they refer to the Italians' vitality and talent for living well.

A non-Italian finds the Italians' apparent fondness for all things foreign and dependence on foreign cultural models (from America above all) an astonishing contrast to the conservatism and inertia of Italian models for living and everyday behavior. More than anything else, foods provide the foreigner with an image of Italian resistance to outside influence.

It is odd that although Italy occupies a predominant position in the invention and production of fashion in the world, no contamination has taken place between the fashion system and the wholly Italy-centered system of foods. That contamination is beginning to occur abroad with Italian restaurants, but in Italy food remains a realm governed by local guarantees (clients trust only the cuisine that has its roots in local traditions) rather than by international applause. In short, in Italy, cuisine has not yet become an industry, a commodity, a consumer good. The values attached to it are not quoted on the stock exchange or represented in international fairs. Publicity does not determine its success. Pasta is advertized, but there is no publicity for cuisine as such. Italian cuisine remains a vernacular sphere, in the sense that it is born within domestic walls or pseudo-domestic ones where the cook is a public version of the Mamma, not a chef. The cook is not a personage, a temperamental keeper of secrets, as he is in England or France, but someone who is approachable because domestic, even if the hearth at which he operates has steel stoves and metal pots and pans.

Hunger and Variety

Variety raises another question. The very variety of types of pasta (and, in part, types of pizza) contains a paradox: How did an undernourished people invent something so very formal and in such an abundance of types?

To be sure, Italy of the late nineteenth century and the first half of the twentieth century was a land in which many people found it hard to find enough to eat. But isn't it incredible that, once the industrial system for the production of dried pasta was put into place, pasta was produced, not in two or three types, but in some six hundred? The culture of poverty in Italy is very often a culture of variety, embracing a thousand types of bread, a thousand ways to cook things, and a thousand types of pasta and pizza.[6] Moreover, that poor culture was much more baroque than a flatly rationalist and functionalist reading of recent Italian history has proved capable of understanding. This has also been true in another sector that is as misunderstood as foodstuffs, popular architecture (so-called "spontaneous architecture"), or the way in which people have resolved the problem of putting a roof over their heads. Italy created a lengthy catalog of forms and decorations in which there are thousands of types and solutions for each region in Italy.

In both cases scholars, historians, folklorists, sociologists of all stripes, and all who speak of the cultures of poverty as cultures of the "defeated," or the "underdog" have displayed their myopia. (It is instructive to look back to advertising campaigns of the 1970s and '80s and see how the term *subalterno* was used to hide an ignorance or prejudice concerning "popular" cultures—another disputable term—as if they were second-rank, cultureless cultures.) Pasta is a slap in the face to those who focus on the essential; the exact contrary of the indispensable minimum, it resolves the problem of too little with variety, not monotony.

---

[6]This variety, amusingly enough, was exported to America in the form of numbers, as anyone who spent his childhood in Brooklyn or the Bronx can attest. You went to the corner grocery store or the neighborhood Mom and Pop store and asked for "number 38" or "number 4," knowing perfectly well that the latter meant spaghettini, not spaghetti, bucatini, or maltagliati.

Sequence

In the history of mealtime, pasta and pizza represent a revolution. They are, as we have seen, an effective solution to the problem of feeding large masses of people. Pasta in my own personal alimentary culture is tied to the memory of some twenty places—some of which remain—surrounding the market squares of Palermo, where you could get a plate of pasta to eat at mid-day. There would be a door you could knock at or a shop that would provide a spoon or fork and a plate of food, eaten standing or sitting on the step in the pause between one moment and another of the day. Late-nineteenth-century prints and early twentieth-century photographs of Naples show the same sort of consumption—at times with the hands—of pasta bought from an ambulant vendor, who added the cheese. Like spaghetti, pizza was also eaten at the market or along the street in that time period.

One difference between pizza and pasta is that although both arose as street foods, one was a dry food with toppings and the other was runny—a difference that determined the more public destiny of pizza as a food to be eaten "out," with the hands and without a plate, whereas pasta, as a more liquid food, found its future at table and was eaten with a fork, becoming the first in the series of courses that make up a meal. Pizza is public, as is often true (as Mary Douglas suggests) of dry foods offered on festive occasions. In Sicily, up to fifty years ago, for example, *scaccio*—dried fruit—was a typical "refreshment" offered at weddings. "Dry" foods go well with the informal life of the piazza or the street, as its more prosaic consumption and its manageability remind us. A plate of drippy pasta demands that the consumer soon seek a place to sit down.

As early as 1832 Melchiore Gioia thundered in the *Nuovo Galateo* that "the use of paws is the exclusive right of the beasts," and if the legend is true, it seems that it was a chamberlain in the court of Franceschiello (Francesco II, king of the Two Sicilies), who invented the three-pronged fork to keep His Majesty, who was enormously fond of spaghetti, from looking like a beast when he ate. The fact remains that pasta, as a good but drippy food, became a dish that should be eaten in intimate circumstances rather than in broad daylight; among family and friends, not in public.

Here we encounter the knotty question of sequence. There is probably a connection between the fact that pizza is eaten with the hands (even by civilized people, Miss Manners or no Miss Manners) and the idea that it is not one course in a series of courses.

Pasta, on the other hand, recalls the domestic hearth and is eaten with a four-tined fork (short pasta with a spoon) with a dexterity learned as a child and aided by sucking in, a natural impulse (as Miss Manners explains). The magnificent Japanese film, Juzo Itami's *Tampopo*, depicts the Nipponese embarrassment of students taking lessons in how to eat spaghetti noiselessly. Japanese good manners and tradition declare that sucking in noisily is part of the correct way to eat rice noodles or wheat noodles.

In any event, the pasta/fork or pasta/spoon relationship places pasta within a ritual sequence in which pasta is served as a first course. Both at home and in a restaurant, pasta is no longer the only dish in a meal. It is a primo that satisfies urgent need ("I'm hungry") but not the need of nourishment (the second course is more substantial).

The pasta system is complicated because pasta is part of a sequence. Moreover, varying the sequence is not allowed and is in fact an infraction that may elicit astonishment. Meat before pasta? Salad maybe, for some devotees of naturism, but the antipasto (literally, "before the meal") or the *hors d'oeuvre* ("outside of the meal") must be an undertone, something out of sequence that must not interfere with the regular sequence of first course—second course—fruit.

Primo, the cook in Stanley Tucci and Campbell Scott's film, *Big Night*, is well aware of this. It is why he gets so angry when an American customer, unenthusiastic about a risotto that she finds not authentically Italian, asks that some spaghetti be put on the same plate. Primo, pushed to his limits, threatens to put mashed potatoes on the plate as well. She has committed a really grave error, not because spaghetti and rice are both carbohydrates (many dishes—*pasta e patate*, for example—combine two carbohydrates), but because they are inappropriate together, a case of "cabbage for a snack," hence an insult. Not everything is permitted, because within any one system of variations and temporal order similar elements such as two or three *primi piatti* on the same plate cannot be superimposed. Doing so is a form of incest, of coupling against nature and against the grain; it countermands the ordered nature of an alimentary system. For this reason one must be careful about projecting onto other cuisines the idea of the proscription of certain food-stuffs (for instance, the alimentary prohibitions or combinations forbidden in Jewish, Islamic, or Marrano cooking), while believing that our own systems do not have just as many internal rules. For an Italian, mixing rice with pasta is like putting salami in milk, eating fruit with pasta, or eating cabbage as a snack. Anyone who does so displays a mental and cultural imbalance because these are infringements of "purity" rules (as Mary Douglas intuits in her comparison of primitive and "developed" societies) that contain the danger of discovering that a given behavior, gesture, or food lies outside the classifications and the orders inherent to a culture. In similar fashion, it is thought dangerous to eat a creature that is neither meat nor fish, or to mix melon with white wine. (Jean-Louis Flandrin has written marvelous pages on the perils attributed to the latter combination, credited with killing more than one pope or monarch.)

The consecrated sequence of *primo-secondo-frutta* is another expression of domestic religion. We go to McDonald's to break the rules, and we come back home to feel at ease again. Sequence is a form of unwritten law that is transcribed in every menu (and in fact a menu is a "table of the law"—better, a "law of the table"—reconfirming the nature of things). Italians find it difficult even to imagine that other cultures do not have a sense as finely tuned as their own of what is appropriate and inappropriate in an alimentary sequence. Moreover, the elements of that sequence are different for *pranzo*—the mid-day meal—and *cena*—the evening meal. It is rare, for example, to see broth as a first course at mid-day, unless it contains ravioli or tortellini.

When we encounter a foreigner stupefied by so much rigidity, we Italians consider him a barbarian, someone who, as Judith Martin's Miss Manners would say, is unaware of even the rudiments of "basic civilization" because he does not know how to use a fork.

Physical Techniques

Nourishing oneself (as distinguished from staving off hunger) is a bodily technique. It requires a skill that does not come naturally, but rather is learned, like walking or talking. It involves a knowledge of how and what to eat, how to use one's arms and hands, how to bring the food to one's mouth, and how to chew it and swallow it. Thus, just as many Oriental peoples learn to use chopsticks from childhood, Italians learn how to twirl spaghetti around a fork, to the point of forgetting that they are doing so. Marcel Mauss tells us that bodily techniques are learned at a tender age and then transformed into automatisms. Taste is also a bodily technique; it is not a simple sense, but rather a training of the senses. For this reason, absolute taste does not exist: what exists is a taste that is based on frequentation, on long familiarity with a context of landscapes, aromas, excesses and faults, spices and evanescences. It is a product of education: one becomes habituated to appreciating the subtle variations of a spate of spices or hot peppers, just as one gets used to tolerating tofu's apparent lack of taste or the strong smell of tripe. Taste is an education, and not only of the palate: it implies vision, touch, and actions, along with the experience of having seen food prepared and having prepared it oneself. We understand this when we go out to eat at an Italian restaurant outside Italy (or even at home) and realize that a dish does not taste as it should. There are no manuals for that "should," and no trustworthy recipes for it. The sardines in *pasta con le sarde* should crunch under the tongue in a certain way; the subtle mix of *finochietto di montagna* (wild fennel) and hints of fish operates within strict, authoritarian limits of tolerance for the dish to be "the way it should be." For similar reasons, a sommelier or a cheese-taster has a nearly impossible job, because with wines and cheeses—but also with every true dish from a local cuisine—there is connection with a specific terrain, with the sun it receives, and with the moment and the circumstances in which such things are eaten or drunk. There are savors that are possible only because they recall others: for example fruit, metal, wood, or stone are all part of the local landscape. To drink or to eat is to inhabit a landscape, to gobble it down for one's pleasure; it is the view of a place made edible. Is it not clear to any native of Southern Italy that *pasta con il pomodoro* is also a landscape, or that the colors of pizza and mozzarella are those of the dawn and the night, humors of the wind, and shades of color?

Thus, just as it is clear that a good part of taste is form, as I stated at the beginning of this essay, it is also true that one can appreciate a landscape, but one cannot know it well unless it is internalized by living in it for quite some time. For this reason, when Louis

Marin or Roland Barthes compare alimentary systems and languages, they are both right and wrong. Barthes tells us that "taste is oral, like language, and liminal, like eros." It is also true, however, that orality and the intimacy of taste are only two of the elements of an inhabited cuisine. There is also memory; there is expectation; there is the result. Dishes are more similar to witty sayings than they are to phonemes; they are compositions that have to have a certain effect and that are offered to the expectation of those who are clever enough to appreciate them and who manage to laugh.

This is why being bi- or pluri-culinary is something rarer and more difficult than being bilingual or pluri-lingual. I hope that this does not offend supporters of multi-culturism, but in general, one can only sample another cuisine, not adopt it as one's own.

Admittedly, creolizations exist, as do creole cuisines. But it takes generations for two or more cuisines to mingle. This seems to be happening now in Australia as Chinese cuisine blends with certain local specialities, and it surely happened in the creole cuisines and in many Afro-American and Aftro-Caribbean cuisines. For the restaurants of some multi-ethnic cities, this is more a matter of contamination or pidginization—that is, they deliberately attempt a *mélange*. Achieving a creole cuisine takes time, and it cannot be taken for granted that something good will emerge. It is also true, however, that entire regional cuisines that we Italians are used to thinking of as "ours" are complicated contaminations from many worlds. Sicilian cooking, for example, includes Sephardic elements, a French fondness for innards, a

North-African taste for sweet and sour, a Middle Eastern idea of grilling, a Swiss habit of using cream in desserts, and the Turkish tradition of sherbert.

Nostalgia?

So, if pasta and pizza belong to a specific culture and are part of a technology of the body learned in infancy, today, with our mass culture and McDonaldization, are they not cultural artifacts on their way to extinction? Is Camporesi perhaps right in lamenting the fact that "fast food" seems to be eliminating all gastronomic delights? And should the news that spaghetti itself is being "McDonaldized" with the opening of chains like "Basta/Pasta" and 'Pasta/Sì" make us sad, nostalgic, or angry? I am not sure. It is probable that there is a loss, as I said earlier in connection with grandmothers and their kitchens. It is probable that our own is one of the last generations with strong memories of a natural use of cooking, a use like a spoken language, or of cuisine as a habit of tastes and ways of doing things that was close to hand, required no reflection, no consultation of a recipe book. Today we are at least in part losing the ability to take that widespread culture for granted, and we can only reacquire it intellectually by reading recipes of all sorts, from the immoral recipes of Vásquez Montalbán to those of Suor Germana.

There is an incredible inertia connected with cultural things, however, and a capacity for latency that can last for decades and generations. Cultural systems, like languages, can seem to disappear, only to return in other forms and at other times. Local languages are vital, in spite of globalization, precisely because systems adapt and readapt to domination in subterranean ways, and they end up by breaking through like grass through asphalt. The marvelous history of creole languages demonstrates this, and it demonstrates to us the highly Italian talent for passing through an entire century of globalization, in fact, galloping through it, with a domesticity sold as universality. We should not forget—and the aim of this book lies precisely here—that the history of pasta and pizza stands as proof that a hundred years are enough to construct an identity and to construct it in the mouth, *al dente*, in such a way as to persuade everyone that it has always existed. ■

Selected Bibliography

Agnesi, Vincenzo. *È tempo di pasta: Scritti 1960-1976* (Rome: Gangemi, 1992).

Alberini, Massimo. "Presentation of Anna Martini, Pasta & pizza" (Milan: Mondadori, 1974), in English translation by Elisabeth Evans as "Introduction," in *Martini, Pasta & Pizza* (New York: St. Martin's Press, 1977).

Artusi, Pellegrino. *La scienza in cucina e l'arte di mangiar bene: Manuale pratica per le famiglie* (Florence, 1891), (Turin: Einaudi, 1995).

Barthes, Roland. Introduction to Brillat-Savarin, *La physiologie du goût, édition mise en ordre et annotée avec une lecture de Roland Barthes; texte établi par Michel Guibert* (Paris: Hermann, 1981).

Basile, Giambattista. *Lo cunto de' li cunti* (1636) edited by Ezio Raimondi; translated, with facing text, by Benedetto Croce (Turin: Einaudi, 1976), in English translation by Sir Richard Burton as *Il pentamerone; or, The Tale of Tales* (New York: Liveright, 1943).

Benincasa, Gabriele. *La pizza napoletana: Mito, storia e poesia* (Naples: Benincasa, 1992).

Biasin, Gian-Paolo. *Biasin, I sapori della modernità: Cibo e romanzo* (Bologna: Il Mulino, 1991), in English translation as *The Flavors of Modernity: Food and the Novel* (Princeton: Princeton University Press, 1993).

Camporesi, Piero. *La terra e la luna: Alimentazione, folclore e società* (Milan, 1989), in English translation by Joan Krakover Hall as *The Magic Harvest: Food, Folklore, and Society* (Cambridge UK: Polity Press, 1993).

Cavour, Camillo Benso, Count. *Lettere edite e inedite di Camillo Cavour.* 6 vols. (Turin: Roux e Favale, 1884-87).

Chamoiseau, Patrick. "Un enfance créole," in *Antan d'enfance* (Paris: Gallimard, 1993), in English translation by Carol Volk as *Childhood—Antan d'enfance* (Lincoln: University of Nebraska Press, 1999).

Di Giacomo, Salvatore. Article in *Corriere di Napoli*, 30 November 1983.

Douglas, Mary. "Food as a System of Communication." In Douglas, *In the Active Voice* (London and Boston: Routledge & Kegan Paul, 1982), in Italian translation as "Il cibo come sistema di comunicazione," in *Antropologia e simbolismo: Religione cibo e denaro nella vita sociale* (Bologna: Il Mulino, 1985).

Dumas, Alexandre. *Le Corricolo* (1843); (Paris: Desjonquières, 2001).

Fante, John. *The Brotherhood of the Grape* (Boston: Houghton Mifflin, 1977; Santa Rosa Cal.: Black Sparrow Press, 1988), in Italian translation as *La confraternita del Chianti* (Milan, 1995; 6th ed., Milan: Marcos y Marcos, 1999).

Foerster, Robert F. *The Italian Emigration of Our Times* (1919) (New York: Arno, 1969).

Goody, Jack. *Cooking, Cuisine, Class: A Study in Comparative Sociology* (Cambridge and New York: Cambridge University Press, 1982).

Illich, Ivan. *Poesie e novelle; Teatro; Cronache,* vol. 1 ed. Francesco Flora; vol. 2 ed. by Mario Vinciguerra (Milan: Mondadori, 1946).

La Cecla, Franco. "Faux contact." In Sophie Bessis, ed., *Mille et une bouches: Cuisines et identités culturelles, Series mutation/mangeurs,* n. 154 (Paris: Autrement, 1995).

--------. *Il malinteso: Antropologia dell'incontro* (Bari: Laterza, 1997), in French translation by Annemarie Sauzeau as *Le malentendu,* foreword by Marc Augé (Paris: Balland, 2002).

Marchi, Cesare. *Quando siamo a tavola* (Milan: Ruzzoli, 1990).

Marin, Louis. *La parole mangée et autres essais théologiques-politiques* (Paris: Méridiens Klincksieck, 1986), in English translation, with an afterword, by Mette Hjort, as *Food for Thought* (Baltimore: Johns Hopkins University Press, 1989).

Marinetti, Filippo Tommaso and Luigi Colombo Fillìa. *La cucina futurista* (1930) (Milan: Longanese, 1986), in English translation by Suzanne Brill as *The Futurist Cookbook* (San Francisco: Bedford Arts, 1989).

Martin, Judith. *Miss Manners' Guide to Excruciatingly Correct Behavior* (New York: Atheneum, 1982).

Maxwell, Lula Beth. "Macaroni History With Food Value Facts..." *Macaroni Journal,* February 15, 1938 (Minneapolis).

Mintz, Sidney W. *Tasting Food, Tasting Freedom: Excursions into Eating, Culture, and the Past* (Boston: Beacon, 1996).

Monelli, Paolo. *Il ghiottone errante: Viaggio gastronomico attraverso l'Italia* (Milan: Fratelli Treves, 1935; Touring Club Italiano, 2005).

----------. See also Sada.

Montanari, Massimo. *La fame e l'abbondanza: Storia dell'alimentazione in Europa* (Bari and Rome: Laterza, 1996), in English translation by Carl Ipsen as *The Culture of Food* (Oxford UK and Cambridge Mass: Blackwell 1994).

Panzini, Alfredo. *Dizionario moderno delle parole che non si trovano nei dizionari comuni* (1905) (Milan: Hoepli, 1950).

Pastario, ovvero Atlante delle paste alimentari italiane, Il, edited by Eugenio Medagliani and Fernanda Gosetti (Lodi: Biblioteca Culinaria, 1997).

Polo, Marco. *The Travels of Marco Polo*, translated from the text of L. F. Benedetto by Aldo Ricci (New Delhi: Asian Educational Service, 2001).

Sada, Luigi. *Spaghetti e compagni: Prima documentatione per una storia delle paste alimentari e nomenclatura dialettale pugliese* (Santo Spirito, Bari: Edizioni del Centro librario, 1982).

Salaparuta, Enrico Alliata, duke of. *Cucina vegetariana e naturismo crudo: manuale di gastrosofia naturale...* (Palermo: Sellerio, 1988).

Scarpi, Paolo. "La rivoluzione dei cereali e del vino: Demeter, Dionysos, Athena," in Oddone Longo and Paolo Scarpi, eds., *Homo Edens: Regimi, miti e pratiche dell'alimentazione nella civiltà del Mediterraneo* (Milan: Diapress/document, 1989).

Sentieri, Maurizio. *Cibo e Ambrosia: Storia dell'alimentazione mediterranea tra caso, necessità e cultura* (Bari: Dedalo, 1993).

Sereni, Emilio. "Note di storia dell'alimentazione nel Mezzogiorno: I napoletani da 'mangiafoglia' a 'mangiamaccheroni'," in Sereni, *Terra nuova e buoi rossi e altri saggi per una storia dell'agricoltura europea* (Turin: Einaudi, 1981).

Soriano, Osvaldo. "Lucio Demare, el tango del Abasto a París," in Soriano, *Artistas, locos y criminales* (Buenos Aires: Bruguera, 1983), in Italian translation as *Artisti, pazzi e criminali* (Turin: Einaudi, 1996).

Tasca Lanza, Anna, with photographs by Franco Zecchin, *The Heart of Sicily: Recipes and Reminiscences of Regaleali, a Country Estate* (London: Cassell and New York: Potter, 1993).

Tognazzi, Ugo. "Una carbonara americana," in Tognazzi, *L'abbuffone* (Milan: Rizzoli, 1974).

Tomasi di Lampedusa, Giuseppe. *Il Gattopardo* (Milan: Feltrinelli, 1958), in English translation by Archibald Coquhoun as *The Leopard* (New York: Pantheon, 1960).

Traglia, Gustavo. *Il lunario della pastasciutta* (Milan: Ceschina, 1956).

Varotti, Adriano. *Il ciclo del mais nell'economia somala: Struttura aziendale e dinamiche socio-economiche nell'agricoltura del Basso Scebeli* (Rome: Gangemi, 1989).

Additional Bibliography

Apicius, *De re coquinaria*, in English translation by Joseph Dommers Vehling as *Cookery and Dining in Imperial Rome* (New York: Dover, 1977).

Archestratus of Gela. *Hedupatheia phagetike.*

Aron, Jean-Paul. *Le mangeur du XIXe siècle* (Paris, 989), in English translation by Nina Rootes as *The Art of Eating in France: Manners and Mores in the Nineteenth Century* (Harper & Row, 1975).

Bessis, Sophie, ed. *Mille et une bouches: Cuisines et identités culturelles, Series mutation/mangeurs,* n. 154 (Paris: Autrement, 1995).

Bruno, Giordano. *Lo spaccio della bestia trionfante*, in English translation as *The Expulsion of the Triumphant Beast* (Lincoln: University of Nebraska Press, 2004).

Corominas, Joan. *Diccionario etimológico della lengua castellana*. 6 vols. (1954); Reprint (Bern: Francke, 1970.

Crosby, Alfred W. *Ecological Imperialism: The Biological Expansion of Europe, 900-1900* (1986). 2nd ed. (Cambridge and New York: Cambridge University Press, 2004), in Italian translation as *Imperialismo ecologico: L'espansione biologica dell'Europa (900-1900)* (Bari and Rome: Laterza, 1988).

De Roberto, Federico. *L'imperio* (Milan: Mondadori, 1929).

Fante, John. *Wait Until Spring, Bandini* (New York: Stackpole, 1938; Santa Barbara: Black Sparrow, 1983), in Italian translation as *Aspetta Primavera, Bandini!* (Milan: Marcos y Marcos, 1995).

Fasano, Gabriele. *Lo Tasso napoletano*: Zoè, La Gierosalemme libberata (1689).

Fiorillo, Silvio. *La Lucilla costante* (1632); ed. Monica Brindicci (Naples: Bellini, 1995).

Flandrin, Jean-Louis. "Mangiare il melone." *Il Mondo* 3, nn. 2-3, August-December 1995.

Foa, Anna. "La cucina del marrano," *Il Mondo* 3, II, nn. 203, August-December, 1995.

Iacocca, Lee A. *Iacocca: An Autobiography* (Toronto and New York: Bantam, 1984).

Ibn al-'Aww m. *The Book of Agriculture.*

Idrisi. *Il libro di Ruggero*, trans. and ed.by Umberto Rizzitano (Palermo: Flaccovio, 1966).

Lalande, Joseph Jérôme de. *Voyage en Italie fait dans les années 1765 et 1766.* 9 vols. (Paris, 1768).

Leopardi, Giacomo. *Zibaldone*, ed. Rolando Damiani. 3 vols. (Milan: Mondadori, 1997).

Maffi, Mario. New York; *L'isola delle colline: I luoghi, la vita, le storie di una metropoli sconosciuta* (Milan: Il Saggiatore, 1995).

Malouin, Paul Jacques. *Les arts des aliments: Comprenant Description et détails des arts du meunier, du vermicelier et du boulanger* (1767); (Bayac: Roc de Bourzac, 1995).

Mauss, Marcel. "Body Techniques." In Mauss, *Sociology and Psychology: Essays by Marcel Mauss* (London: Routledge & Kegan Paul, 1979), 95-123.

Prezzolini, Giuseppe. *Maccheroni & C.* (Milan: Longanesi, 1957)

Scaraffia, Lucetta. "Regole alimentari e identità religiosa," *Il Mondo* 3, II, nn. 2-3, August-December 1995).

Scarpi, Paolo. "La rivoluzione dei cereali e del vino: Demeter, Dionysos, Athena." In Oddone Longo and Paolo Scarpi, eds., *Homo Edens: Regimi, miti e pratiche dell'alimentazione nella civiltà del Mediterraneo* (Milan: Diapress/document, 1989).

Serventi, Silvano, and Françoise Sabban. *La Pasta: Storia e cultura di un cibo universale* (Rome and Bari: Laterza, 2000), in English translation by Antony Shugaar as *Pasta: The Story of a Universal Food* (New York: Columbia University Press, 2002).

Spadaccino, T., ed., *La Sicilia dei Marchesi e del Monsù* (Palermo, 1996).

Suor Germana, with the collaboration of Enrica Chiapparelli. Marmellate, conserve, liquori, 2nd ed. (Casale Monferrato: Piemme, 1991).

Theophano, Janet Schwarz. "It's Really Tomato Sauce But We Call It Gravy: A Study of Food and Women's Work Among Italian American Families." PhD diss. University of Pennsylvania, 1982.

Vásquez Montalbán, Manuel, *Recetas immorales* (Barcelona: Dolce Vita, 1988).

Also available from Prickly Paradigm Press:

Paradigm 1 *Waiting for Foucault, Still*
Marshall Sahlins

Paradigm 2 *War of the Worlds: What about Peace?*
Bruno Latour

Paradigm 3 *Against Bosses, Against Oligarchies: A Conversation with Richard Rorty*
Richard Rorty, Derek Nystrom, and Kent Puckett

Paradigm 4 *The Secret Sins of Economics*
Deirdre McCloskey

Paradigm 5 *New Consensus for Old: Cultural Studies from Left to Right*
Thomas Frank

Paradigm 6 *Talking Politics: The Substance of Style from Abe to "W"*
Michael Silverstein

Paradigm 7 *Revolt of the Masscult*
Chris Lehmann

Paradigm 8 *The Companion Species Manifesto: Dogs, People, and Significant Otherness*
Donna Haraway

Paradigm 9 *9/12: New York After*
Eliot Weinberger

Paradigm 10 *On the Edges of Anthropology (Interviews)*
James Clifford

Paradigm 11 *The Thanksgiving Turkey Pardon, the Death of Teddy's Bear, and the Sovereign Exception of Guantánamo*
Magnus Fiskesjö

Paradigm 12 *The Root of Roots: Or, How Afro-American Anthropology Got its Start*
Richard Price and Sally Price

continued

Paradigm 13 *What Happened to Art Criticism?*
James Elkins

Paradigm 14 *Fragments of an Anarchist Anthropology*
David Graeber

Paradigm 15 *Enemies of Promise: Publishing, Perishing, and the Eclipse of Scholarship*
Lindsay Waters

Paradigm 16 *The Empire's New Clothes: Paradigm Lost, and Regained*
Harry Harootunian

Paradigm 17 *Intellectual Complicity: The State and Its Destructions*
Bruce Kapferer

Paradigm 18 *The Hitman's Dilemma: Or, Business, Personal and Impersonal*
Keith Hart

Paradigm 19 *The Law in Shambles*
Thomas Geoghegan

Paradigm 20 *The Stock Ticker and the Superjumbo: How The Democrats Can Once Again Become America's Dominant Political Party*
Rick Perlstein

Paradigm 21 *Museum, Inc.: Inside the Global Art World*
Paul Werner

Paradigm 22 *Neo-Liberal Genetics: The Myths and Moral Tales of Evolutionary Psychology*
Susan McKinnon

Paradigm 23 *Phantom Calls: Race and the Globalization of the NBA*
Grant Farred

Paradigm 24 *The Turn of the Native*
Eduardo Viveiros de Castro, Flávio Gordon, and Francisco Araújo

Paradigm 25 *The American Game: Capitalism, Decolonization, World*
             Domination, and Baseball
             John D. Kelly

Paradigm 26 *"Culture" and Culture: Traditional Knowledge and*
             Intellectual Rights
             Manuela Carniero da Cunha

Paradigm 27 *Reading* Legitimation Crisis *in Tehran: Iran and the*
             Future of Liberalism
             Danny Postel

Paradigm 28 *Anti-Semitism and Islamophobia: Hatreds Old and New*
             in Europe
             Matti Bunzl

Paradigm 29 *Neomedievalism, Neoconservatism, and the War on Terror*
             Bruce Holsinger

Paradigm 30 *Understanding Media: A Popular Philosophy*
             Dominic Boyer

Paradigm 31 *Pasta and Pizza*
             Franco La Cecla